THE

GREAT CHEFS®

COOK

ITALIAN

Authentic Italian Recipes and Dishes of Italian Inspiration

Cooked in America's Finest Restaurant Kitchens

More than 100 Recipes from Antipasti to Zabaglione Adapted from

the Recipes Demonstrated on the "Great Chefs®" Television Series and Videos

COMPILED AND EDITED BY ELLEN BROWN

An Ellen Rolfes Book

MAIN STREET BOOKS/DOUBLEDAY

NEW YORK LONDON TORONTO SYDNEY AUCKLAND

A Main Street Book
PUBLISHED BY DOUBLEDAY
a division of Bantam Doubleday Dell Publishing Group, Inc.
1540 Broadway, New York, New York 10036

Main Street Books, Doubleday, and the portrayal of a building with a tree are trademarks of Doubleday, a division of Bantam Doubleday Dell Publishing Group, Inc.

Library of Congress Cataloging-in-Publication Data
The great chefs cook Italian / edited by Ellen Brown. — 1st ed.
        p.   cm.
    ISBN 0-385-47866-6
    1. Cookery, Italian.   I. Brown, Ellen.
TX723.G758   1995
641.5945—dc20   95-22788
                                                          CIP

Printed in the United States of America

October 1995

1   2   3   4   5   6   7   8   9   10

First Edition

Design: Barbara Cohen Aronica

CONTENTS

There are some simple skills involved in making your own pasta, roasting peppers, or peeling tomatoes, and these skills can be transferred to the recipes in any book after reading this primer on Italian techniques.

First courses in Italian restaurants are antipasti—literally "before the pasta." This chapter contains a wide range of foods and flavors, from simple Marinated Eggplant or Asparagus with Tomato Basil Coulis to an ocean full of delicious fish and shellfish dishes and such classics as Carpaccio of Sirloin done with an American twist.

While most Italians eat pasta as a separate course, Americans tend to view this popular food as a one-dish meal. Many great pasta dishes, such as Two-Salmon Pasta or Linguine with Seafood, require almost as little time to make the sauce as it takes the water to come to a boil. And rich risotto, creamy from careful tending, is a blank canvas for a myriad of flavoring.

FISH AND SEAFOOD ENTRÉES WITH AN ITALIAN ACCENT
83

Since Italy is a peninsula, many varieties of fish and shellfish are harvested on its coasts. This chapter includes recipes that enhance the delicacy of aquatic species native to Italy, as well as recipes that transfer the flavors of Italian food to American favorites, such as soft-shell crabs and oysters.

POULTRY AND GAME BIRD ENTRÉES: SIMPLE AND SPLENDID
105

While the Italian kitchen produces many chicken dishes, both in Italy and in the States, chefs are more likely to opt for the heartier members of the fowl family, from succulent capon to hearty duck. This chapter contains easy but elegant recipes like Capon with Rosemary and Scaloppine of Chicken with Stir-Fried Vegetables as well as Grilled Marinated Quail and Roasted Squab with Bacon and Sage to save for special occasions.

MEAT AND GAME ENTRÉES FOR ALL SEASONS
127

Veal is the meat most often served by Italian chefs, and many Americans have also discovered that its tenderness and ability to cook quickly makes it as appealing to serve as its delicacy. While hearty Ossobuco or Roasted Sausages and Grapes might be a welcome warming on a cold winter night, lighter fare such as Veal Piccata or Grilled Veal Chops are wonderful in summer as well.

ITALIAN LITTLE TOUCHES
157

A simple grilled steak served with the mélange of vegetables known as Caponata, or with Fried Eggplant, can create an Italian-inspired meal from almost any dish, and this chapter contains the recipes for some of these small dishes, conceived by chefs as part of larger plate presentations, that are worthy of being served separately.

DESSERTS: LA DOLCE VITA
177

Italian desserts run the gamut of ingredients and levels of formality. While there are many simple fruit desserts, such as Strawberries Italian Style or Raspberry and Fig Gratin, Italian desserts also include the universal favorite—chocolate—as well as many custards flavored with wines and spirits.

MAIL ORDER SOURCES
203

INDEX
205

FOREWORD

How lucky the next generations of Americans will be to have access to the visual record, filmed as part of the "Great Chefs" television series and videos, of hundreds of famous chefs working in their kitchens. While we can only imagine the precision with which Escoffier worked in his kitchen, we can see chefs of his caliber from a United Nations of backgrounds creating feasts before our eyes.

During the past twelve years, individual cities highlighted in the thirteen-part "Great Chefs" series included Chicago and San Francisco as well as two looks at New Orleans, a city that embraces eating out as a passion. After those series, Great Chefs' executive producer John Shoup and director John Beyer changed format and began looking at regions with the twenty-six-part "Great Chefs of the West," "The New Garde," and "Great Chefs of the East."

In addition to the series, many single-subject home videos have been released, ranging in topics from "A New Orleans Jazz Brunch" to "A Holiday Table Cookbook" and "Seafood Sampler."

The quest for culinary prowess has led from the rocky coast of Maine to the beaches of Southern California, and in addition to restaurant chefs, traditional American celebrations such as a clambake on Nantucket Island and a Texas barbecue have been recorded for the enjoyment of today and the posterity of tomorrow.

As the author of both *Southwest Tastes*, the book that accompanies "Great Chefs of the West," and *Great Chefs of the East* I have served as a translator between chefs and home cooks, testing and writing recipes to work in our kitchens.

Since these books accompany their respective series or videos, the recipes had to be presented as the chefs prepared them. This is not the case, however, in *Great Chefs Cook Italian*. The recipes have been streamlined and shortened to keep them within the time constraints of the contemporary home cook.

Chefs do not worry about advance preparation since they have a team to prepare everything *à la minute*. Home cooks, however, want to be part of their parties, so each recipe has been analyzed to give tips on how much of a dish can be prepared how far in advance.

For the books that I did not write, my editing process has included adding expanded directions to many recipes; this is intended to clarify terms chefs use that are not part of the home cooks' basic skills. I have also added, at the front of the book, many basic recipes and techniques that are common to many recipes. These range from stocks—the "secret ingredient" of why chefs' soups and sauces have such depth of flavor—to a basic pasta dough that can be made very quickly.

The recipes in this book reflect a spectrum of Italian and Italian-inspired recipes consistent with today's quest for flavor, variety, and convenience.

Ellen Brown
Nantucket, Massachusetts

INTRODUCTION: ITALIAN FOOD, ITALIAN-AMERICAN FOOD, AND ITALIAN INSPIRATION IN NEW AMERICAN CUISINE

What we know today as traditional American foods were based on prototypes brought by Western European settlers prior to the Civil War. French bouillabaisse became transformed into Cajun gumbo by the Acadian settlers of the bayous, as the Spanish turned their paella into jambalaya in the same region, and the English tradition of double-crust pies held firmly from New England to Virginia.

When later immigrant groups, such as the Italians, Eastern Europeans, and Chinese, arrived in large numbers in the late nineteenth century, they settled primarily in large cities, and their native foods were less likely to be absorbed into the already established mix of dishes then known as American.

The Italian influence on American cooking began in this manner, with trattorias in New York's Little Italy, Boston's North End, and San Francisco's North Beach serving fare adapted to American ingredients and eaten primarily by Italian-Americans and their families until the twentieth century.

More than 80 percent of the Italians who immigrated to the United States in the decades following the Civil War came from the area south of Rome, particularly from Naples and Sicily. This was the region of Italy that adopted the tomato after its introduction from America in the sixteenth century, and most of the dishes in this poor agrarian region were vegetarian.

The Italian-Americans longed for the foods of their homeland, but while dried pastas could be imported, they found it necessary to substitute ingredients indigenous to the United States for many of the originals. One of the major differences in Italian-American cooking from that of Italy is the amount of meat included. Meatballs were added to spaghetti; layers of meat and sausage were combined with the cheese in lasagne, and veal dishes became standards. Steaks and chops, served alone or treated with Italian-style sauces, appeared on the menu along with items such as clams casino, invented by a waiter in New York, and turkey Tetrazzini, named for an Italian opera singer.

Menu items many Americans believed were Italian, such as fettuccine Alfredo, pasta primavera, shrimp scampi, and veal parmigiano, were not native to any province in Italy, but were the inventions of chefs at restaurants who adapted authentic fare to appeal to a larger audience of Americans not of Italian descent.

At the lower level of Italian-American restaurants were the pizzerias, based on a then-little-known Neapolitan bread. One step up were small restaurants featuring red-checked tablecloths and the ubiquitous Chianti bottles. These restaurants, located in Italian areas of major cities, drew their clientele not just from true Italians (who were just as likely to eat at each other's homes as at a restaurant), but from a variety of ethnic groups.

Only a few Italian-American restaurants began to rival French cuisine for what was considered elegant ethnic dining in major cities. Sardi's and Mama Leone's became landmarks for tourists to New York, and Madame Galli's in Chicago, which opened in 1883, was the site of the founding of the national Rotary Club.

It was the Blue Moon Café in San Francisco's North Beach that added cioppino to the Italian-American list of dishes. And near New Orleans, Mosca's used fish from the Gulf of Mexico to create an Italian offshoot of Creole cooking (already an amalgam of French and Spanish cuisines). This Italian influence on the cooking of Louisiana is perhaps the strongest thread among the current group of New American chefs updating the foods of that region.

Italian-American fare grew dramatically outside the ethnic community after World War II, as returning soldiers recalled dishes encountered in Europe and wanted to share these palate memories with their families and friends.

When air transportation made European vacations affordable in both time and money to more Americans, they ate in Italy and realized that few restaurants on this continent were producing authentic fare with simply sauced pastas, grilled veal and poultry dishes, panfried seafood, and a cornucopia of magnificent produce.

It was only in the late 1970s that restaurants reflecting authentic Italian cuisine—especially that of the Northern provinces—and fresh rather than dried pastas began opening in great numbers. Spots such as Galileo in Washington, D.C., San Domenico and Felidia in New York, and Rex in Los Angeles drew rave reviews from critics. The food was luxurious, including ingredients like the prized white truffles of Piedmont, and wine lists that went far beyond Chianti in raffia-clad bottles.

American chefs were among the tourists who flocked to Italy in the 1970s and 1980s, and many realized how similar in concept the simple, fresh dishes of Italy were to what they were attempting to create with the lightened fare we now call New American Cuisine.

Without question, "yuppie pizzas and pastas" took hold first in California and became the staples of California cuisine, first defined by food writer Diane Rossen Worthington in 1982.

It was at about the same time that Wolfgang Puck fired his first pizzas in front of diners at Spago in Los Angeles and Alice Waters added innovative pastas to the casual menu at her Chez Panisse Café upstairs from her more formal Provençal restaurant in Berkeley. It was from his years in the kitchen at Chez Panisse that Jeremiah Tower included Italian-inspired dishes on the menu at his primarily Southwestern Santa Fe Bar & Grill in Berkeley.

Chefs all around the country have adopted this new definition of Italian-American food by using ingredients such as heady balsamic vinegar, sun-dried tomatoes, fresh pastas, roasted garlic, and sautéed vegetable sauces for pasta.

Since American chefs are not bound by the regional definitions and dishes of authentic Italian cuisine, they have absorbed the influences and ingredients not only from Italian provinces but from other Mediterranean countries as well.

Chefs such as George Germon and Johanne Killeen opened Al Forno in Providence, Rhode Island, proving that one need not be Italian-born to have an appreciation for the aesthetic of the food. While Al Forno and similar restaurants are primarily Italian, many stars of the New American constellation have absorbed Italian influences to lesser degrees.

Jimmy Sneed uses the ravioli format for a dish featuring succulent Chesapeake Bay scallops at his Frog and The Redneck in Richmond, Virginia, and Charles Palmer serves polenta beside his soft-shell crabs at Aureole in New York.

The recipes in this book encompass all of these influences—the authentic Italian, the traditional Italian-American, and the influences of both on the dishes we now term New American Cuisine.

BASIC
TECHNIQUES
AND RECIPES

*Every cuisine has some basic procedures that are repeated
often as part of many dishes, and Italian and Italian-
inspired recipes are no exception. Pasta dough is formed
and rolled similarly—regardless of the nuances of the
recipes—and foods such as bell peppers need to be roasted
and peeled for everything from salads to soups and sauces.
This chapter is designed to explain with some depth these
basics of cooking. If you already know how to accomplish
them, then the cross-references in the individual recipes
can be ignored. Once these skills are mastered, there
are worlds of dishes that will be within your grasp.
There are also some basic recipes, such as those for
stocks, that are integral to all cuisines. What
differentiates restaurant soups and sauces is the
depth of flavor created by long-simmered stocks that
are no more difficult to create than boiling water.*

Carefully rinse artichokes under cold running water to remove any grit. Time permitting, it's best to soak them in warm salted water for 1 hour to draw out insects or grit.

Trim the stems to 1 inch or less so that the artichoke can stand upright. Pull off the lower outer petals. Break off any tough outer leaves and trim the tips of the leaves with scissors.

To save time, slice off the top inch of the cone leaves with a heavy knife. Cut off the top $1/2$ inch of the remaining leaves with kitchen shears.

To prevent discoloration, either dip the artichoke in a solution of 1 tablespoon of lemon juice per quart of water placed in a stainless steel or glass bowl, or immediately rub the top and bottom with lemon juice.

Artichokes should be cooked in enamel or stainless steel pans; aluminum will give them a metallic taste.

Handling Bell Peppers

Bell peppers now come in a rainbow of colors, and there are literally hundreds of varieties of chiles. Here are some general rules common to all:

How to cut: Most recipes for bell peppers and chiles specify "seeds and ribs removed." While traditionally this required a paring knife to cut out the ribs, the following method is like sculpting in relief. You cut away the edible portion, leaving a skeleton of ribs and seeds to discard.

Cut a slice off the bottom of the pepper, so that it will stand firmly on the cutting board. You will see the ribs indenting the contour of the pepper. Holding the cap with your free hand, slice down the natural curvature of the pepper in sections. You will be left with all the pepper and none of the seeds and ribs. The flesh can now be cut as indicated in the recipe.

How to peel: Many recipes calling for bell peppers bury the line "roasted, peeled, seeded, and . . ." in the ingredients list. Achieving perfect roasted peppers is a two-part process involving heating and then cooling them, so the skin separates from the flesh.

For recipes like pepper salad, in which the peppers should retain firmness, it is better to roast and chill them quickly. For recipes such as a sauce in which the pepper is puréed, more tender peppers are desirable.

For all peppers, cut a small slit near the stem end with the tip of a paring knife to insure that they will not explode.

Here are ways to heat them:

- For a large number of peppers, and to retain the most texture, lower them gently into 375°F. oil and fry until the skin blisters. Turn them with tongs when one side is blistered, since they will float on the surface of the oil. This method is also the most effective if peppers are not perfectly shaped, since it is difficult to get the heat from a broiler into the folds of peppers.
- Place the peppers 6 inches from the broiler element of the stove, turning them with tongs until all surfaces are charred.
- Place the peppers 4 inches above a hot charcoal or gas grill, and turn them until the skin is charred.
- Place a wire cake rack over a gas or electric burner set at the highest temperature, and turn the peppers with tongs until all surfaces are charred.
- Place the peppers on a rack on a cookie sheet in a 550°F. oven until totally blistered. Utilize this method only for a sauce or other recipe in which the peppers are to be puréed.

For cooling peppers, the options are not as plentiful:

- Place them in ice water. This stops the cooking action immediately, and cools them enough to peel them within a minute.
- The alternative is to wrap the peppers in a plastic bag and allow them to steam. This also effectively separates the flesh from the skin, but it will be 20 minutes or longer before they are cool enough to handle, and they soften during that time.

There are no choices to make for the final step: Pull the skin off, remove the seeds, and rinse the peppers under cold water.

To Make Beurre Blanc Sauce

In the days of French nouvelle cuisine, white butter sauces replaced traditional white sauces as the chefs' darling. They actually contain far more fat than a white sauce, although they appear to be lighter on the palate.

4 shallots, peeled and finely chopped
¹/₂ cup white wine
¹/₂ cup white wine vinegar
2 tablespoons heavy cream
1 pound (4 sticks) unsalted butter
Salt and freshly ground white pepper

Combine the chopped shallots, wine, and vinegar in a skillet or sauté pan, and place over high heat. Cook, stirring occasionally, until only 2 tablespoons of liquid remain in the pan. Then stir in the cream, and reduce the heat to low.

While the liquid is reducing, cut the butter into 1-tablespoon pieces.

Using a wire whisk, add the butter, 1 tablespoon at a time, swirling the pan over the heat as you whisk it in. The sauce should be kept hot enough so that steam rises from the surface, but not so hot that there is any boiling action. Gradually continue to incorporate all the butter, waiting until each piece has melted in and giving the sauce a chance to reheat for about 10 seconds before adding the next piece. Season with salt and pepper to taste, and serve immediately.

M AKES 2 CUPS OF SAUCE, ENOUGH TO SERVE 8

HANDLING CHOCOLATE

Chocolate is not difficult to work with if preliminary steps are taken to melt it on low heat so that it is satiny. If chocolate has a white film—called a "bloom"—it will disappear after it has melted; the "bloom" is some of the cocoa butter.

To chop chocolate: Chopping it into fine pieces makes melting easier. This can be done in a food processor fitted with the steel blade. Begin by breaking it with a heavy knife rather than breaking it with your hands. Body heat is sufficiently high to soften the chocolate so it will not chop evenly.

To melt chocolate: This can be done in a number of ways (with all of these methods, melt until the chocolate is just about smooth, since the heat in the chocolate will complete the process):

In the top of a double boiler placed over barely simmering water; in the microwave oven by placing chopped chocolate in a microwave-safe bowl and microwaving on 100 percent (HIGH) for 20 seconds, then stir and repeat as necessary; or by heating the oven to 250°F., placing the chopped chocolate in the oven, and then turning off the heat immediately. Stir after 3 minutes, and return to the warm oven if necessary.

To Clarify Butter

The easiest way to clarify butter is to melt it over low heat, then cover and refrigerate it. Once the fat has hardened, you can scoop it off, being careful to leave the bottom layer of milk solids. Store the clarified butter, covered, in the refrigerator or freezer; it will hold in the refrigerator for up to two weeks.

If you don't have time to allow it to chill, melt the butter gently so the milk solids will settle at the bottom of the pan, forming a creamy white sediment. The very thick middle layer is pure butterfat. Carefully and slowly pour off the clear, yellow butter and discard the milk solids.

To Prepare Soft-shell Crabs

Some fish stores will have the crabs already cleaned; however, it is not difficult to do it yourself. Turn the crab on its back. Pull off the triangular apron. Lift up the side flaps and pull out the spongy fingerlike gills. With scissors, cut off the face just behind the eyes. Gently press above the legs and pull out the bile sac. Soft-shell crabs are delicious cooked on a grill, either marinated or brushed with butter. They are most often sautéed or pan-fried, first dusted with seasoned flour or batter, for about 3 to 5 minutes per side.

To Pick Crabmeat

Already packaged crabmeat is far from perfect in many cases. There are bits of shell and cartilage that must be removed. Spread the crab out on a dark-colored plate, and many fragments will become obvious to pick out. Then carefully rub the morsels between your fingers, being careful not to break up the large lumps.

To Make Contemporary Demi-glace

While traditional demi-glace, which as been around since the seventeenth century, is thickened with flour so it must simmer gently with much tending, this quick version is much lighter and can be made more quickly since it is only thickened at the end with arrowroot or cornstarch.

The key to demi-glace is rich, unsalted homemade stock, and the demi-glace should taste like the base from which the stock was made—roasted veal and/or beef, or browned chicken. All of the other flavorings are subtle and secondary.

2 tablespoons vegetable oil
1 large onion, peeled and diced
2 stalks celery, peeled and diced
1 carrot, scrubbed, trimmed, and sliced
½ cup diced ham
3 tablespoons tomato paste
1 sprig thyme
1 bay leaf
6 peppercorns
10 cups brown veal stock
½ cup Madeira
2 to 3 teaspoons arrowroot mixed with 2 tablespoons cold water
Salt and freshly ground black pepper
1 tablespoon unsalted butter

Heat the oil in a large saucepan over medium heat. Add the onion, celery, carrot, and ham, stir, and cover the pan. Cook over low heat for 10 minutes to sweat the vegetables. Uncover the pan and stir in the tomato paste, thyme, bay leaf, and peppercorns. Whisk in the stock and Madeira, and bring to a boil over high heat.

Once the mixture has started to boil, it can boil rapidly over medium-high heat. The faster it boils, the more quickly it reduces. Cook the sauce until only 2 cups of liquid remain; depending on the rate at which the liquid is boiling, this can take anywhere from 30 minutes to 1 hour. When you think the sauce has reduced sufficiently, strain it into a measuring cup. If it has not reduced enough, pour the reduction back into the pot and keep boiling. If it has reduced too much, add enough water to reach 2 cups.

Place the strained sauce back in the pan and bring it back to a simmer. Stir in the arrowroot mixture a little at a time until the sauce reaches the desired consistency. (Reduction sauces thicken from the process alone, so add the arrowroot slowly and wait until the sauce returns to a simmer and thickens before adding any more arrowroot.)

Finishing the sauce: If you are using the sauce immediately, season with salt and pepper. The last step is swirling in the butter, which will give the sauce a satiny appearance and a richer flavor.

If you are not serving immediately, season, but do not whisk in the butter; remove the pan from the heat and place dots of butter on the surface of the sauce to prevent a skin from forming. Whisk the butter in when reheating the sauce.

MAKES 2 CUPS

HANDLING GARLIC

Fresh garlic can range in flavor from powerful to soft and mellow, depending on how the cloves are treated. Garlic has no aroma until it is cut and an enzyme is released, and it is a general rule that raw garlic is always more aromatic and pungent than cooked garlic.

To slice: For recipes that will simmer for a long period, sliced garlic is easy and flavorful. Simply peel and slice lengthwise into thin pieces.

To mince: Peel the garlic, and slice lengthwise with a very sharp knife. Keeping the garlic together, make a quarter turn and slice again. Continue to chop the garlic, using a rocking motion with your knife. Hold the tip end with your other hand and use quick, small strokes. As the garlic spreads out, use the knife to push it back to the center. Keep chopping until the garlic is very fine.

To roast: Roasted garlic has a nutty, sweet flavor, and enhances many dishes, from soups to mashed potatoes. Rub a whole head of garlic with a teaspoon of olive oil. Place in a 375°F. oven loosely wrapped in foil for 45 minutes. Cool until warm enough to handle.

Separate the cloves and press out the pulp by pinching the top of each clove; the soft pulp will emerge from the stem end.

Procedures for Grilling

Prepare the fire at least 30 minutes before you want the food to start cooking, with the vents totally opened at the bottom of the grill. For quick lighting, use a chimney starter with crumpled newspaper in the bottom and briquettes or charcoal above. Or stack the charcoal in a pyramid shape and light with a liquid or electric starter following the manufacturer's instructions.

Once the coals are lit, spread them evenly to be sure of uniform cooking and prevent charring. Before placing the food on the grill, check the temperature of the fire. Thin items such as steaks, chops, burgers, or boneless chicken breasts require a hot fire, while for whole pieces of chicken and thicker meat the fire should be medium hot. Vegetables should be cooked over a medium fire since they have no fat to lubricate them.

Here are the terms used to describe a fire:

- Hot: The coals are still showing red glare, and you can hold your hand at grill level for only 2 seconds.
- Medium-hot: The coals are lightly covered with gray ash, and you can hold your hand at grill level for 3 to 5 seconds.
- Medium: The coals are totally covered with gray ash, and you can hold your hand at grill level for 6 to 7 seconds.

To use wood chips: Soaking aromatic wood chips in water and placing them on the hot coals can add additional flavor to grilled food. When using wood chips, place them only on a hot or medium-hot fire, since the moisture will cool the coals down quickly. (When you grill foods uncovered, the chips will not give the same flavor impact as when you use the cover on the grill.)

Handling Fresh Herbs

The first step in using herbs is to strip them from the stems. Large leaves should be plucked off one by one, and small leaves can be sheared off between your thumb and index fingernails, starting at the base of the sprig and moving upward.

Use your discretion as to including bits of stem. While bits of tender thyme stem are not worth the bother of stripping too carefully, a rosemary stem can be as tough as eating a log.

Chopping fresh herbs: Except when used whole as a garnish, or for tiny leaves such as thyme, most herbs are chopped, in one of a few ways:

Using a food processor: Strip the leaves from the stems and put them in the food processor. Chop using on and off pulsing action until the desired consistency is reached.

Using a chef's knife: Pile the leaves on a cutting board. Cut the herbs into small pieces, holding the tip of the blade against the board and rocking the handle up and down until they are the desired size, scraping them into a pile to keep chopping them evenly. Make sure the knife is very sharp or you will bruise the herbs rather than cut them.

Cutting fresh herbs: Creating thin slices, called a *chiffonade* in French cooking, only works with herbs such as basil and sage that have large leaves. Stack the leaves on a cutting board, and roll them tightly lengthwise. With a small paring knife, cut across the rolled bundle of leaves in thin strips.

To Make Hollandaise Sauce

Like mayonnaise, hollandaise can be made successfully in a blender or food processor fitted with the steel blade. The trick is to make sure the butter is hot enough to heat the egg yolks, since they are not being heated by direct heat.

1¹/₂ **cups unsalted butter**
6 egg yolks
¹/₃ **cup hot water, just below a simmer**
3 to 4 tablespoons freshly squeezed lemon juice
Salt and freshly ground white pepper

Place the butter in a saucepan and melt over medium heat until bubbly and hot. Set the water to heat in a small saucepan. While the butter is melting, beat the egg yolks in a blender or food processor until thick and lemon-colored, for about 1 minute. As the egg yolks are beating, remove the water from the flame. Slowly add the water through the tube, and beat until the mixture is thick.

Slowly add the hot butter to the egg yolk mixture. Add the first quarter of the butter in drips; then add it in a very thin stream. If the butter seems to be cooling, place it over the heat for 30 seconds. When the fat has been added, discard the milky whey.

Stir in the lemon juice, and season with salt and pepper to taste.

To make by hand: Making hollandaise in the top of a double boiler—the time-honored method—takes far too long. Here is a faster way:

Melt butter as above. Whisk the egg yolks in a heavy-bottomed saucepan, with $^1/_3$ cup cold water. Place the pan over medium-high heat and whisk constantly until the mixture thickens and expands in volume. Remove from the heat, and whisk for 30 seconds to cool it. Then, while whisking constantly, add the hot butter a few tablespoons at a time. Finish as above.

MAKES 2 CUPS

TO CLEAN LEEKS

Trim the top of the leek, leaving some green, or remove it altogether, depending on the recipe. Discard the outer leaves and trim the root. Split the leek in quarters or halves almost through the root, depending on size. Rinse the leek down to the root in cold water, shaking it to loosen any dirt, and reassemble the layers for cooking.

If the leeks are going to be sliced or chopped, it is easier to do this before cleaning and then place them in a colander and rinse well, tossing them with your fingers to remove any grit.

TO TOAST NUTS

Spread the nuts in a single layer on a shallow pan or baking sheet with edges. Bake at 350°F., shaking the sheet occasionally until the nuts are golden, 5 to 12 minutes, depending on size. Leave them to cool.

To toast nuts on the stove: While nuts will brown in the oven without additional fat, if you brown them in a frying pan, they should be toasted over low heat in a little butter or oil, depending on the recipe. Watch them carefully, since they can scorch easily.

HANDLING FRESH OYSTERS

Oysters in the shell will need to be cleaned. Scrub the oyster thoroughly under cold tap water, using a brush. Never submerge oysters or any shellfish in plain water or they will suffocate.

There are several ways to open an oyster and with a little practice you can become skilled at the art of shucking. For easiest shucking, use an oyster knife, a pointed can/bottle opener, or a screwdriver. Protect your hands by wearing heavy-duty rubber gloves or enclose the oyster in several thicknesses of a folded kitchen towel.

Shucking by hand: Hold the shell in the palm of your hand with the deeper side down to preserve most of the oyster liquor.

Locate the hinged part of the oyster (the narrow end), and with a back-and-forth motion gently work the tip of the oyster knife between the shell halves.

Once the knife has penetrated the shell (by $1/4$ inch or so), make sure the oyster is firmly impaled on the blade by giving the shell a few shakes. It should remain firmly stuck on the end of the knife. Working very carefully, twist the knife back and forth to open the shell.

Once the shell is opened, slide the knife across the top of the shell to cut the adductor muscle and run the knife under the body of the oyster. Discard the top shell.

The microwave method: Place the oysters in a glass casserole dish. Put them in microwave for 5 minutes on WARM (30 percent). Remove from the oven, pry open, and shuck at once. Using this method, the oysters will be uncooked, and should be placed on a bed of ice to chill well before serving.

You can completely open oysters by putting them in the microwave for 3 minutes on HIGH (100 percent). The oysters will be thoroughly cooked.

The oven method: Heat the oven to 400°F. and scrub the oysters. Place the oysters on a cookie sheet on a rack in the middle of the oven for 5 minutes. Have ready a dishpan or sink full of ice water.

Immediately dump the oysters into the chilled water. The hinges will pry open easily.

Handling Dried Pasta

With the increasing sophistication of Italian food in North America, we are coming full circle and realizing that supple fresh pastas are not the best match for many hearty sauces, and there is always a place in the pantry for a box of spaghetti or penne. Good-quality dried pasta is made with a high percentage of high-gluten semolina, the inner part of the grain of hard durum wheat. The gluten gives the pasta resilience, and allows it to cook while remaining somewhat firm, the elusive al dente.

There are virtually hundreds of authentic pasta shapes in Italian cuisine, and many can be substituted for one another. The best guide for substitution is to look at the chart below and seek a pasta with a similar cooking time and use to the one specified in a recipe.

A GUIDE TO DRIED PASTAS

NAME AND MEANING	DESCRIPTION	COOKING TIME	USES
Anelli, Rings	Medium-small, ridged, tubular pasta cut in thin rings	6 to 8 minutes	Soups
Cannelloni, Large Pipes	Large cylinders	8 to 10 minutes with further baking	Stuffed with cheese or meat sauced, and baked
Capellini, Hair	Very fine, solid, cylindrical; the finest is capelli d'angelo (angel's hair)	2 to 4 minutes	With oil, butter, tomato, seafood, or other thin sauce; soup
Cavatappi, Corkscrews	Medium-thin, hollow, ridged pasta twisted into a spiral and cut into short lengths	8 to 10 minutes	With medium and hearty sauces
Farfalle, Butterflies	Flat, rectangular noodles pinched in center to resemble butterfly or bow; may have crimped edges; farfalline are tiny butterflies	10 to 12 minutes	With medium or hearty sauces; baked; soups
Fettuccine, Little Ribbons	Long, flat, ribbon-shaped about 1/4 inch wide	6 to 9 minutes	With medium heavy, rich sauces (e.g., Alfredo)
Fiochetti, Bows	Rectangles of flat pasta curled up and pinched slightly in the center to form bow shapes	10 to 12 minutes	With medium and hearty sauces
Fusilli, Twists	Long, spring- or corkscrew-shaped strands; thicker than spaghetti	10 to 12 minutes	With tomato and other medium-thick sauces
Lasagne	Large, flat noodles about 3 inches wide; usually with curly edges	6 to 8 minutes with baking	Baked with sauce, cheese, and meat or vegetables
Linguine, Little Tongues	Thin, slightly flattened, solid strands, about 1/8 inch wide	6 to 9 minutes	With oil, butter, marinara, or other thin sauces

NAME AND MEANING	DESCRIPTION	COOKING TIME	USES
Maccheroni, Macaroni	Thin, tubular pasta in various widths; may be long like spaghetti or cut into shorter lengths	8 to 10 minutes	With medium and hearty sauces
Manicotti, Small Muffs	Thick, ridged tubes; may be cut straight or on an angle	8 to 10 minutes	Filled with meat or cheese and baked
Mostaccioli, Small Mustaches	Medium-sized tubes with angle-cut ends; may be ridged (rigatti)	7 to 10 minutes	With hearty sauces
Orecchiette, Ears	Smooth, curved rounds of flat pasta; about 1/2 inch in diameter	6 to 8 minutes	With oil and vegetable sauces or any medium sauce; soups
Orzo, Rice Pasta	Tiny, grain-shaped	7 to 10 minutes	Soups or braised in stock
Pastini, Tiny Pasta	Miniature pasta in any of various shapes, including stars, rings, alphabets, seeds/teardrops	3 to 4 minutes	Soups, or buttered as a side dish with or without Parmesan cheese
Penne, Quills or Pens	Same as mostaccioli	10 to 12 minutes	With hearty sauces
Rigatoni	Thick, ridged tubes cut in lengths of about 1 1/2 inches	10 to 12 minutes	With hearty sauces; baked
Rotelle, Wheels	Spiral-shaped	7 to 10 minutes	With medium or hearty sauces
Spaghetti, Little Strings	Solid, round strands ranging from very thin to thin; very thin spaghetti may be labeled spaghettini; wheat flour	8 to 12 minutes	With oil, butter, marinara, seafood, or other thin sauces
Tagliatelle	Same as fettuccine; may be mixed plain and spinach noodles, called paglia e fieno (straw and hay)	6 to 9 minutes	With rich, hearty sauces
Vermicelli, Little Worms	Very fine cylindrical pasta, similar to capellini; wheat flour	4 to 7 minutes	With oil, butter, or light sauce

NAME AND MEANING	DESCRIPTION	COOKING TIME	USES
Ziti, Bridegrooms	Medium-sized tubes; may be ridged (rigati); may be long or cut in approximately 2-inch lengths (ziti tagliati)	10 to 12 minutes	With hearty sauces; baked

Try to purchase pasta that you can see behind cellophane in a box. The pasta should be smooth and shiny, not crumbly.

Store pasta in sealed plastic bags once the boxes are opened. Pasta will stay fresh for at least six months. If it is stale, the cooking time will be slightly longer but it can still be used.

A large quantity of salted water and careful timing are the keys to properly cooked pasta. For one pound of dry pasta, use a six-quart pot, preferably a tall one. Fill it with four to five quarts of water, and bring the water to a boil. Add two scant tablespoons salt, and stir with a wooden spoon. When the water is bubbling vigorously, drop in the pasta all at once. When you cook spaghetti or other long pasta, push it in with your hand and, with the aid of a wooden spoon or fork, submerge it completely in the water. Stir with a wooden spoon or fork to prevent the strands from sticking together.

Cover the pot briefly to bring the water back to boil quickly. Remove the cover, and slightly lower the heat to prevent the water from boiling over. Stir the pasta from time to time.

Packages of pasta usually provide cooking instructions; however the time listed is frequently too long. Begin to test the pasta several minutes before the minimum cooking time.

Al dente does not mean raw or hard. The pasta should be firm but not rigid or stiff, presenting some resistance to the bite without being hard. If you break it with your fingers and the inner core is still white, it isn't done. When the pasta is al dente, stop the cooking by turning off the heat and pouring one cup of cold water into the pot.

Drain the pasta in a colander immediately, and shake briskly a couple of times to remove all the excess water.

Regardless of the sauce you are using, it must be ready when the pasta is done. If the pasta is not tossed with the sauce immediately, it continues to cook while it sits. It's a good idea to reserve one cup of the cooking water in case you need to dilute the sauce.

When you cook two pounds of pasta, it isn't necessary to double the amount of water; increase it by 1 or 2 quarts.

Pasta yields:

1 serving = 3 to 4 ounces dried

3 to 4 ounces dried = 2 to $2^{1}/_{2}$ cups cooked, depending on the shape

1 pound dried = 4 to 6 servings

MAKING FRESH PASTA

The formula for fresh pasta may be thought of as the "base" recipe to produce a stiff dough that can be stretched, rolled into thin sheets, and then cut into the desired shape.

The flour for fresh pasta should be bread flour so that the higher protein count will give the pasta the resiliency to be rolled, and will keep that slight bite of al dente when cooked.

For flavored pastas, there are spinach and tomato flours on the market; however it is unnecessary to buy these extra ingredients and the flavor is not as strong as when fresh ingredients are added when mixing the pasta.

BASIC PASTA DOUGH

1 pound ($3^{1}/_{2}$ cups) bread flour
2 tablespoons olive oil
5 eggs
$^{1}/_{4}$ teaspoon salt

There are three basic ways to mix pasta dough:

Mixing by hand: Combine the dry ingredients on a clean work surface and make a well in the center. Place the liquid, eggs, flavoring ingredients, and oil in the well, and working as rapidly as possible, gradually incorporate the flour into the liquid ingredients until a loose mass is formed. Knead the dough vigorously until it becomes smooth and elastic.

Mixing in a food processor: Place all the ingredients in the work bowl of a food processor fitted with the steel blade. Process the ingredients until they are blended and the dough resembles a coarse meal. To test for the proper consistency, pinch a small amount of the dough. If it does not clump together easily, it is too dry. Add a small amount of water, process the dough again briefly, and check it again. If the dough is too wet, it will form a ball that rides on top of the blade. Add a small amount of flour and process the dough again briefly. Remove the dough from the processor and gather it into a ball. The dough should feel slightly moist but not tacky.

Mixing with an electric mixer: This is a job for heavy-duty countertop mixers only; do not try it with a hand mixer, since the dough is too thick for the mixer to operate effectively. Place all ingredients in the work bowl of the mixer, and using a dough hook, blend the ingredients at medium speed until the dough forms a smooth ball that pulls cleanly away from the bowl.

For all methods: Allow the dough to rest, covered with plastic wrap, for at least 1 hour before rolling it out.

After the dough has been allowed to rest, it can be rolled into sheets, either by hand or by machine. The resting stage is particularly important if the dough is to be rolled by hand, since if it is not sufficiently "relaxed," it will be difficult to roll into thin sheets.

Rolling by machine: Different machines will have different methods of operation. The guidelines below are intended for use with a two-roller hand-operated machine.

Working with no more than one-fifth of the dough at a time, with the rollers set at the widest opening, begin to guide the dough through the machine. Fold the sheet in thirds, like a letter, and run in through the rollers again. Repeat this step two or three times, folding the dough into thirds each time. If necessary, dust the dough with flour to keep it from sticking to the rollers.

Continue to roll the pasta through the machine, setting the rollers at a narrower setting each time, until the sheet of pasta is the desired thickness. If necessary, lightly dust the sheets with flour to prevent them from sticking or tearing.

Allow the pasta to dry before cutting it. The dough should feel smooth and not at all tacky. Ideally, the pasta sheets should be draped to dry in such a way that air can reach both sides at once. The sheets should not be overdried, because the dough can become brittle and difficult to cut.

Cut the pasta as desired, by hand or using attachments for the machine.

Rolling by hand: Flatten a manageable amount of dough (about the size of an orange) on a clean work surface dusted with flour. Using a rolling pin, work from the center of the dough to the edges with a back-and-forth motion, rolling and stretching the dough. Continue rolling, turning the dough occasionally and dusting it with flour to prevent sticking and tearing, until the sheet is the desired thickness.

Dry and cut it as outlined above.

Cooking fresh pasta: Fresh pasta can be kept refrigerated prior to cooking for up to two days. If the pasta is cut in long strands, it should be sprinkled with cornmeal or semolina to keep the strands from sticking together. Refrigerate the pasta on trays lined with plastic wrap, and cover it with plastic wrap as well.

If fresh pastas are to be stored for more than two days, they can be allowed to dry in a warm, dry area and then may be held, well wrapped, in a cool, dry spot in the same manner as commercially prepared dry pastas.

Fresh pasta cooks very quickly, and should not be left unattended once added to the pot.

Bring a large amount of water to a rolling boil. The ratio of water to pasta is 4 quarts of water for 1 pound of pasta. Add salt to the water, if desired. Add the pasta, and stir it to separate the strands or shapes.

It's best to cook long pastas in a colander that can be submerged into the pot and drawn out immediately as soon as the pasta is ready.

For filled pastas, reduce the heat to a simmer to keep them from breaking apart or bursting open.

Drain the pasta in a colander (unless a pasta cooker is being used) and serve it immediately with the sauce.

One pound fresh pasta yields 3 to 4 servings.

FRESH PASTA FLAVORINGS PER 1 POUND OF FLOUR

Pasta Type	Additional Ingredients/Adjustments
Spiced Pasta	2 to 4 teaspoons ground spices such as a combination of cumin and coriander
Spinach Pasta	½ cup cooked, puréed spinach and 4 eggs
Saffron Pasta	Mix 2 teaspoons crushed saffron threads with the eggs
Citrus Pasta	2 tablespoons lemon or orange zest
Herb Pasta	¼ to ½ cup chopped fresh herbs
Black Pepper Pasta	2 to 4 teaspoons coarsely cracked black peppercorns added to the eggs
Red Pepper Pasta	⅔ cup puréed, roasted red bell pepper and 4 eggs
Tomato Pasta	¼ cup tomato paste and 4 eggs
Carrot Pasta	½ cup cooked, puréed carrots and 4 eggs
Beet Pasta	½ cup cooked, puréed beets and 4 eggs

HANDLING PHYLLO DOUGH

Phyllo is a paper-thin pastry that becomes crisp and brown when brushed with fat and baked. It is the basis for Greek and Middle Eastern dishes such as spanakopitta and baklava, and can be used for Eastern European strudels. In contemporary cooking, chefs are using phyllo in a free-form manner to create anything from a crunchy topping for basic casseroles to dessert bundles, and it is replacing puff pastry in all except classic French cooking.

Almost any recipe calling for puff pastry can be made with phyllo dough, and it will be lighter and crispier.

Although it varies by brand, a package of phyllo contains approximately 18 to 24 sheets, each sheet measuring about 12 by 20 inches. The phyllo should be defrosted completely for at least 8 hours at room temperature before opening. It can also be defrosted in a microwave oven at MEDIUM (50 percent) power; take it from the outer carton but leave the inner plastic pouch sealed. Defrost for 3 to 5 minutes, depending on the power of the microwave.

When handling phyllo, you will need to work as quickly as possible, so it is important to have all ingredients ready. If using only part of the dough at a time, cover the remaining phyllo with a slightly damp towel or plastic wrap, or put the phyllo that you aren't immediately using in the refrigerator, tightly wrapped in plastic wrap.

For almost all dishes using phyllo, the sheets must be brushed with some sort of fat. For many dishes, such as strudels and baklava, the layers of phyllo are also separated by a dry mixture.

For sweet phyllo dishes, unsalted clarified butter should be used to coat the sheets. It is important to clarify the butter to remove the milk solids, since they can make the phyllo soggy. Do not use salted butter; even though some of the butter leaches out during baking, the salt does not, and the amount of salt in most salted butter will render the finished dish too salty. It will take approximately 1 pound of clarified butter to treat 1 pound of phyllo.

For a savory dish, the fat coating can be clarified butter or a combination of clarified butter and oil.

For sweet dishes, the dry mixture is usually the following: For each pound of phyllo use ½ pound of nuts, toasted in a 350°F. oven for 5 to 7 minutes and finely chopped, and 2 cups of crumbs. These can be bread crumbs or ground butter cookie crumbs. Sugar, cinnamon, or other flavorings may be added.

For savory dishes, use plain or flavored bread crumbs. Parmesan cheese, dried herbs, or spices may be added.

To Make Stocks

Delicious soups, sauces, and stews are partially the result of long-simmered stocks that add richness and depth of flavor to these categories of dishes, and require the culinary skill of knowing how to boil water.

There are two basic categories of stocks—white stocks and brown stocks. While chicken stock can be either, meat stocks are always the latter and fish or vegetable stocks are the former.

For white stocks, start the main ingredient in the stockpot first with the water, and bring to a boil. Reduce the heat to simmer. For the first 10 or 15 minutes, a foamy gray scum will rise to the top of the pot. This should be removed with a spoon and discarded. Simmer the main ingredient alone for the first hour of cooking. Then add the vegetables and seasonings, and cook to the total time listed below in the recipe.

For brown stocks, preheat the oven to 400°F. Place the bones and trimmings in a roasting pan, and roast in the center of the oven for 45 minutes, turning occasionally and regulating the heat so they do not burn. Then add the vegetables to the pan, and continue to roast for 20 minutes more.

Place the bones and vegetables into a deep stockpot and pour off any accumulated fat. Add 1 quart of the water to the roasting pan and place on the stove over high heat. Stir until the brown bits clinging to the bottom of the pan are incorporated into the water. Pour this into the stockpot with the remaining water specified in a recipe, and bring to a boil over medium high heat. When the stock begins to boil, reduce the heat so that it is barely simmering, and skim the surface of the scum that will rise for the first 10 or 15 minutes.

Some recipes for stock call for the hot stock to be ladled through a sieve lined with cheesecloth to remove all the impurities. Whether or not stock requires straining depends on its ultimate use. For most soups and stock reduction sauces, merely removing the solids from the pot with a slotted spoon or Chinese wire mesh spoon is sufficient. For a crystal-clear stock, it's handier to use a paper coffee filter than cheesecloth.

Stock should be left at room temperature until cool before refrigerating. Once refrigerated, any layer of fat on poultry or meat stocks can be easily skimmed off and discarded. Stocks can remain refrigerated, tightly covered, for up to five days.

CHICKEN STOCK

6 quarts water
5 pounds chicken bones, skin, trimmings
2 carrots, scrubbed, trimmed, and cut into chunks
1 large onion, peeled and halved
3 cloves garlic, peeled and halved
3 celery stalks, washed and halved
3 sprigs fresh thyme, or 1 teaspoon dried
6 sprigs fresh parsley
3 bay leaves
12 black peppercorns

Bring the water to a boil with the chicken over medium-high heat. Follow the method outlined above. Cook for 1 hour.

Add the vegetables, along with the thyme, parsley, bay leaves, and peppercorns to the pot, and raise the heat until the stock begins to boil again. Reduce the heat once again, and simmer the stock for 3 hours. Follow the method above for straining and chilling.

MAKES 3 QUARTS

MEAT STOCK

8 pounds meat bones and trimmings (veal bones are best)
2 onions, peeled and halved
2 carrots, scrubbed, trimmed, and halved
2 stalks celery, washed and halved
3 cloves garlic, peeled and halved
8 quarts water
3 sprigs fresh thyme
6 sprigs fresh parsley
2 bay leaves
12 peppercorns

Follow the method above for brown stock. Simmer the stock for 5 to 6 hours, then strain out the solids and discard. Cool and degrease the stock as outlined above.

MAKES 3 QUARTS

FISH STOCK

4 quarts water
1 cup dry white wine
4 pounds fish trimmings (including skin, skeletons, shellfish shells, lobster bodies broken apart, heads)
2 tablespoons lemon juice
1 onion, peeled and halved
2 stalks celery, washed and halved
4 sprigs fresh parsley
2 sprigs fresh thyme
6 peppercorns

Bring the water and wine to a boil over high heat. Wash all the fish trimmings, and bring to a boil with the water and wine, following the method described above. Cook for 1 hour.

Add the lemon juice, onion, celery, parsley, thyme, and peppercorns to the pot. When the water returns to a boil, reduce the heat so that it is barely simmering, and simmer for 1½ to 2 hours. Strain the stock, extracting as much liquid as possible from the solids. Discard the solids, and allow the stock to reach room temperature before refrigerating or freezing.

M A K E S   3   Q U A R T S

VEGETABLE STOCK

4 large leeks, trimmed and carefully washed
2 large carrots, peeled and sliced
4 large celery stalks, washed and sliced
4 large yellow onions, peeled and sliced
5 garlic cloves, peeled
6 sprigs fresh parsley
4 sprigs fresh thyme, or 1 teaspoon dried
2 bay leaves
4 quarts water
½ teaspoon white peppercorns
1 teaspoon black peppercorns
Salt

Place all the ingredients except the salt in a deep stockpot. Slowly bring the liquid to a boil over medium heat, and follow the method outlined above. Reduce the heat to low, and simmer, partially covered, for 1½ hours. Add salt once the stock has been strained.

M A K E S   3   Q U A R T S

The taste of summer, vine-ripened tomatoes are an antidote to any heat the season may bring. Tomatoes are easy to prepare for cooking, but some attention should be given to achieve the best results.

To peel tomatoes: Initially, cut out the core of the tomato. With a knife, lightly crosshatch over the bottom of the tomato. Plunge into boiling water and boil for exactly 10 seconds. Remove with a slotted spoon to a bowl of cold water. This change in temperature damages the layer of cells just below the skin, allowing the skin to slip off easily.

To seed tomatoes: Slice the tomato in half through the middle. Squeeze gently over a bowl, and most of the seeds should loosen and drop. Any clinging seeds can be removed with the tip of a paring knife or your finger.

Chopping or dicing: Cut the tomato in half. Seed, then slice into strips and then cut the strips crosswise into a dice.

Using canned tomatoes: These are already peeled, but they still require seeding, and should be drained well before using. The juice can be saved to use in stocks. An easy way to chop them is to place them in a bowl and squeeze them between your hands.

ANTIPASTI
TO
ANTICIPATE

*The antipasti in Italian restaurants frequently greet
diners as they enter the restaurant, with trays of
colorful vegetables cooked or dressed raw in an
attractive manner, along with displays of sausages
and cheeses. For a buffet dinner, a selection of vegetable
dishes that can be made in advance create as stunning
a display on your table as they do in restaurants.
Included in this chapter are some of those dishes, as well as
stand-alone appetizers, salads, and soups. Freshness of the
ingredients is the key to the taste achieved in Italy, so cook
these dishes when the ingredients are in season, so they will
be their most perfect as well as most affordable.*

EMPRESS MUSHROOMS

ADRIANA GIRAMONTI, MILL VALLEY, CALIFORNIA

If mushrooms are past their prime, peel the skin off the caps, using a sharp paring knife, and they will look white and pristine on the plate.

16 medium mushrooms
About $1/2$ cup olive oil
1 small onion, peeled and chopped
1 garlic clove, peeled and minced
6 ounces prosciutto, finely chopped
2 teaspoons minced parsley
2 teaspoons minced fresh marjoram
Freshly ground black pepper
$1/2$ cup white wine
$1/4$ to $1/3$ cup plain bread crumbs
$1/4$ cup grated Parmesan cheese

Preheat the oven to 375°F. Clean the mushrooms thoroughly, then remove and chop the stems. Heat $1/4$ cup of the olive oil in a medium sauté pan over medium heat. Add the onion and garlic and sauté, stirring frequently, for 3 minutes, or until the onions are translucent.

Add the chopped mushroom stems, prosciutto, parsley, marjoram, and pepper to the pan, and sauté for 2 minutes. Add the wine and cook over high heat until the liquid has reduced by two-thirds. Remove the pan from the heat, and stir in enough bread crumbs to bind the vegetables.

Brush the mushroom caps with some of the remaining olive oil, and place them in an ovenproof baking dish. Divide the filling among the mushrooms, sprinkle with cheese, and bake for 5 to 7 minutes, depending on the size of the mushroom. Serve hot or at room temperature.

NOTE: The filling can be prepared up to 1 day in advance and refrigerated, tightly covered. Bring to room temperature before stuffing the mushrooms.

SERVES 4

ARTICHOKES ROMAN STYLE

ADRIANA GIRAMONTI, MILL VALLEY, CALIFORNIA

Artichokes are a favorite Italian appetizer, especially in Rome, and these have extra flavor from the seasoning with which they are cooked, so no sauce is necessary.

12 small artichokes (or 4 large artichokes, cooked for 45 minutes)
Juice of 1 lemon
2 medium onions, peeled and quartered
1 garlic clove, peeled and chopped
1 teaspoon dried marjoram
¹/₄ cup olive oil
1 cup chicken broth
Salt and freshly ground black pepper

Remove the outer leaves of the artichokes, cut off the tops, and let the artichokes stand in cold water with the juice of the lemon for 10 minutes. Arrange the artichokes around the sides of a heavy casserole. Put the quartered onions in the middle. Add the garlic, marjoram, olive oil, broth, salt, and pepper.

Cover the casserole and bring to a boil over high heat. Simmer gently, covered, over low heat for 20 minutes, or until the bottoms of the artichokes are tender when pierced with a tip of a paring knife. Serve hot, or at room temperature.

NOTE: The artichokes can be prepared up to 1 day in advance and refrigerated. Allow them to reach room temperature before serving.

SERVES 4

ARTICHOKE AND HEARTS OF PALM SALAD

ANDRÉ POIROT, NEW ORLEANS, LOUISIANA

This salad with a tangy citrus dressing combines the Italian influence of artichokes with other ingredients and looks as colorful as confetti.

CITRUS VINAIGRETTE
2 tablespoons fresh lemon juice
2 tablespoons fresh orange juice
¼ cup red wine vinegar
½ cup salad oil
1 tablespoon minced shallot
Salt and pepper
1 teaspoon sugar

SALAD
1 cup (3 ounces) quartered white mushrooms
6 to 8 cooked artichoke hearts plus the tender inner leaves (page 8)
1 cup sliced or julienned hearts of palm (one 16-ounce can)
1 cup julienned peeled carrots (about 4 carrots)
4 cups radicchio, leaves separated and cut into shreds
16 cherry tomatoes, stemmed and quartered

To make the vinaigrette, whisk all the ingredients together until emulsified.

To make the salad, combine the mushrooms, artichoke hearts, hearts of palm, carrots, and ³/₄ cup of the citrus vinaigrette in a salad bowl. Let stand for 1 hour.

Line the rims of 4 plates with the artichoke leaves. In the center of each plate place ¹/₂ cup of radicchio. Atop the radicchio, place one-fourth of the marinated vegetable mixture on each portion. Garnish with cherry tomatoes and drizzle a little of the remaining vinaigrette over the artichoke leaves.

NOTE: The vegetables can all be prepared up to 6 hours in advance and refrigerated. Do not marinate the mixture for more than 1 hour, however, or the flavor will become too strong.

SERVES 4

CHEF'S TIP

Artichokes do not pair well with wine, since they contain cynarine, which causes food eaten immediately afterward to take on a sweet taste. This is why it's preferable to serve the artichokes as a course by themselves. If wine is served, try a strong white wine, served very cold.

ASPARAGUS WITH TOMATO BASIL COULIS

JOEL GOURIO DE BOURGONNIER, NEW ORLEANS, LOUISIANA

The fragrant tomato basil mixture is a perfect foil for the plain sautéed aspara-gus with its grassy flavor. This dish is simple yet elegant, and not too rich, but interesting.

4 shallots, peeled and minced
10 garlic cloves, peeled and minced
$^1/_2$ cup plus 1 tablespoon olive oil
5 tomatoes, peeled (page 30)
$^3/_4$ cup V-8 juice, or tomato juice
1 tablespoon chopped fresh parsley
2 tablespoons chopped fresh basil
Salt and freshly ground pepper
1 cup dry white wine
1 bunch (1$^1/_2$ pounds) asparagus, trimmed
2 tablespoons unsalted butter

GARNISH
10 chives, cut into 1-inch lengths
$^1/_4$ cup minced green onions
12 whole fresh basil leaves

In a skillet, sauté the shallots and garlic in 1 tablespoon of the olive oil for 2 minutes, or until soft. Quarter 3 of the tomatoes and add to the garlic and shallots. Add the V-8 juice, parsley, and basil. Season with salt and freshly ground pepper to taste. Cook for 5 to 7 minutes over medium heat, or until heated through.

Pour the mixture into a food processor or blender. Pour the wine into the pan and cook and stir over medium heat to remove any cooked juices from the bottom of the pan. Add this wine to the blender or processor and purée the mixture. With the motor running, add the remaining ½ cup olive oil in a slow, steady stream and process for 2 minutes.

Bring a large pot of salted water to a boil, and add the asparagus. Boil for 2 minutes, then drain and plunge into a bowl of ice water to stop the cooking action.

In a large 10-inch sauté pan, melt the butter and sauté the asparagus for 4 to 5 minutes, or until tender-crisp.

To serve, cover 4 plates with the tomato coulis. Arrange 5 asparagus spears in a fan over the coulis. Mince the remaining 2 tomatoes and arrange equal portions at the base of the asparagus. Garnish with chives, green onions, and fresh whole basil.

NOTE: The coulis can be prepared and the asparagus can be blanched up to 4 hours in advance, and kept at room temperature. Sauté the asparagus just prior to serving.

SERVES 4

CHEF'S TIP

To ensure freshness, cut the ends from the stalks and stand the asparagus in a couple of inches of cool water until ready to clean and cook.

WARM SALAD OF ASPARAGUS AND ARTICHOKE

DANIEL BOULUD, NEW YORK, NEW YORK

A most unusual salad for a first course, aromatic from a mixture of fresh herbs, tart from a triple dose of lemon, this can become an entire meal if accompanied by poached fish or roasted poultry.

4 large globe artichokes

3 tablespoons olive oil

16 asparagus spears, boiled for 2 minutes, drained, and cut into 2-inch pieces

1 red bell pepper, roasted, peeled, seeded, and cut into ¼-inch slices (pages 8–9)

1 yellow bell pepper, roasted, peeled, seeded, and cut into ¼-inch slices (pages 8–9)

2 lemons

4 cups fresh assorted herbs (tarragon, green and purple basil, dill, cilantro, chervil, chives, chicory, parsley, and celery leaves)

Salt and freshly ground black pepper

1 cup halved cherry tomatoes

2 tablespoons basil-infused oil (available at specialty food stores)

Bring a large saucepan of salted water to a boil. Remove all of the large bottom leaves of the artichokes, leaving the cone in the center. Trim the base of any green parts, and cut off the soft cone. Put the artichoke bottoms into the boiling water and simmer, covered, for 15 to 20 minutes, until tender when pierced with a knife. Drain and scoop out the hairy choke. When they are cool enough to handle, slice into ½-inch slices.

Heat 2 tablespoons of the olive oil in a medium sauté pan or skillet over medium heat. Add the artichoke slices, asparagus, and red and yellow peppers. Cook for 2 minutes over medium heat and set aside.

Scrape the zest from one of the lemons with a zester, and squeeze the juice from the lemon. In a large bowl, toss the fresh herbs with the lemon juice, zest, and the remaining 1 tablespoon of olive oil. Season the salad with salt and pepper. Add the cherry tomatoes and toss. Squeeze the juice from the remaining lemon, and pull the pulp out of the rind, discarding the seeds. Purée the pulp and juice in a blender or food processor, and set aside.

To serve, arrange the warm artichokes, asparagus, and peppers on 4 serving plates. Top the vegetables with the herb salad. Sprinkle the puréed lemon pulp and juice over the salad. Drizzle the basil oil around the vegetables.

NOTE: The artichokes can be cooked 1 day in advance and refrigerated, tightly covered. The vegetables can be sautéed up to 6 hours in advance; complete the dish just prior to serving.

SERVES 4

MARINATED EGGPLANT

ADRIANA GIRAMONTI, MILL VALLEY, CALIFORNIA

This is a wonderful variation on the traditional Italian fried eggplant, since the dressing makes it a combination salad and appetizer. Since it can be done in advance, it is a great dish for a buffet dinner.

1 eggplant
4 eggs
1 or 2 teaspoons chopped parsley
Salt and freshly ground black pepper
2¹/₂ cups olive oil
¹/₂ cup all-purpose flour, for dredging
3 garlic cloves, crushed
6 bay leaves
1 teaspoon dried rosemary (optional)
¹/₂ cup red wine vinegar

FRANCESCO RICCHI
CHEF AND OWNER OF I RICCHI, WASHINGTON, DC

Why did you become a chef?
At the age of ten I began following step by step someone who was so dedicated to the job that when the time came for me to decide my future, the decision was already made. The person I followed was my grandmother.

How did you receive your training?
When the time came to take command in the kitchen, I went to work for other chefs that I admired. From each one of them I learned a lot. The bottom line is, no matter how much you already know, you are always learning.

Any tips to pass on?
Read all the recipes you want, but always try to come up with your own interpretation. Follow your own style and do it your own way.

Cut the eggplant into slices about ¼ inch thick. Arrange on dish-towels side by side, sprinkle with salt, let rest 10 minutes, and wipe dry. Reserve.

Beat the eggs with the parsley, a pinch of salt, and pepper in a bowl. Heat half the olive oil (1¼ cups) in a large sauté pan or skillet over medium-high heat. Flour the eggplant slices lightly, then dip in the egg wash. Sauté in the hot oil until golden brown, about 2 minutes on each side. Drain on paper towels.

Meanwhile pour the remaining 1¼ cups olive oil and the crushed garlic into a heavy saucepan. Sauté until the garlic is golden. Remove from the heat and add the bay leaves, rosemary (if using), red wine vinegar, and salt and pepper to taste, then simmer 1 minute. Reserve.

In a bowl with a lid, assemble 1 layer of eggplant, then sprinkle with the simmered garlic marinade. Add another layer of eggplant and sprinkle with marinade. Continue the process until all the eggplant is used; then pour the remaining marinade over the entire dish. Cover, then turn upside down to mix in the marinade. Marinate for at least 2 hours at room temperature. Unmold on a serving plate and serve at room temperature.

NOTE: The dish can be made up to 3 days in advance and refrigerated. Allow it to come to room temperature before serving.

SERVES 4 TO 6

CHEF'S TIP

Eggplants have male and female gender, and the males are preferable, since they have fewer seeds and are less bitter. To tell a male from a female, look at the stem end. The male is rounded and has a more even hole, and the female hole is indented.

PROSCIUTTO DE PARMA SALAD

MICHAEL UDDO, NEW ORLEANS, LOUISIANA

Salads are a highlight of any Italian trip, and that influence is now woven into the menu of Chef Uddo's restaurant in New Orleans. The combination of salty, toothsome prosciutto with tangy cheese and crunchy greens is easy to prepare and exciting to eat.

2 Belgian endives
1 cup frisée
2 cups mâche
1 head radicchio
3¹/₂ ounces prosciutto de Parma, sliced paper-thin
1¹/₂ ounces Romano cheese (Parmesan may be substituted)
2 tablespoons coarsely ground black pepper
³/₄ cup extra-virgin olive oil

Gently pull the endive leaves off the cores, and tear the larger leaves in half. Wash, drain, and chill all the greens. Remove the core from the radicchio, cut into quarters, and chill. Cut the prosciutto into strips and set aside. Shave the Romano into thin pieces and place in a large salad bowl. Add the greens, radicchio, prosciutto, black pepper, and extra-virgin olive oil. Toss and serve, or arrange on the plate in a radial design with the prosciutto in the center.

SERVES 4

CHEF'S TIP

If frisée cannot be located, the same color, flavor, and texture can be achieved with the inner core of a head of curly endive.

CELERY AND WATERCRESS SALAD WITH ANCHOVY DRESSING

CLAUDE AUBERT, NEW ORLEANS, LOUISIANA

The world is divided into people who like anchovies and those who don't. If you are part of the former camp, this is a simple salad with a combination of mild flavors that all take well to the salty, assertive fish.

2 bunches watercress
1 celery stalk, julienned
6 mushrooms, julienned
1 carrot, julienned
1/2 onion, peeled and thinly sliced
2 tablespoons anchovy paste
1 teaspoon Dijon mustard
2 garlic cloves, peeled and minced
2 tablespoons red wine vinegar
6 tablespoons olive oil
2 tablespoons minced fresh parsley
Salt and freshly ground black pepper

Rinse the watercress and discard the tough ends of the stems. Arrange the watercress in a bowl with the celery, mushrooms, carrot, and onion. Combine the anchovy paste with the mustard, garlic, vinegar, olive oil, and parsley. Whisk well, and season with salt and pepper to taste.

Pour the dressing over the salad, and serve immediately.

NOTE: The salad and dressing can both be prepared up to 2 hours in advance and chilled separately. Do not dress the salad until just prior to serving.

SERVES 4

SALAD PRIMAVERA

CHRIS KERAGEORGIOU, NEW ORLEANS, LOUISIANA

SALAD
1 head romaine lettuce, quartered
1 head endive, quartered
1 head Boston lettuce, quartered
1 tomato, chopped
1 leek (white part only), julienned
1 yellow zucchini, julienned
1 red onion, julienned
1 green zucchini, julienned
1 carrot, julienned
8 broccoli florets, boiled for 3 minutes
8 cauliflower florets, boiled for 3 minutes
2 sprigs fresh basil, chopped
2 sprigs fresh parsley, chopped
1 sprig fresh rosemary, chopped

VINAIGRETTE
1 tablespoon Dijon mustard
1/4 cup red wine vinegar
1/4 cup lemon juice
1 sprig fresh basil, chopped
1 1/2 cups olive oil
Salt and coarse black pepper

Arrange quarter sections of romaine, endive, and Boston lettuce on 4 individual salad plates. Add a quarter of the chopped tomato to each plate. Refresh all the julienned vegetables and chopped herbs in ice water. Drain on towels and add to the salad plates.

Whisk the mustard, vinegar, lemon juice, and basil together. Slowly pour in the olive oil while whisking. Season to taste.

Drizzle the vinaigrette on the salads and sprinkle with salt and coarse ground pepper.

NOTE: The salad can be prepared and plated up to a few hours in advance and refrigerated, covered with plastic wrap. Remix the dressing before serving.

SERVES 4

PANCETTA SALAD

DANIEL BONNOT, NEW ORLEANS, LOUISIANA

This delicious salad is simplicity itself, with the flavor derived from the pancetta fat and walnut oil, and garlic-scented croutons topping the crisp greens.

8 slices stale Italian bread
2 garlic cloves, peeled and halved
$^{1}/_{4}$ pound pancetta or bacon
1 head romaine lettuce, rinsed and cut into $^{1}/_{2}$-inch pieces
2 bunches watercress, rinsed and stemmed
$^{1}/_{2}$ cup walnut oil
$^{1}/_{4}$ cup red wine vinegar
$^{1}/_{4}$ cup raspberry vinegar
Salt and freshly ground black pepper

Preheat the oven to 375°F. Rub the slices of bread with the garlic cloves, cut into $^{1}/_{2}$-inch cubes, and toast in the oven for 5 to 7 minutes, or until browned. Set aside.

Cut the pancetta or bacon into rough pieces and cook in a skillet for 3 to 4 minutes, or until the fat is rendered and the pieces are crisp. Remove from the pan with a slotted spoon and set aside.

Put the greens in a bowl and add the walnut oil and bacon drippings, tossing to coat. Deglaze the bacon pan with the red wine vinegar and reduce slightly. Pour this over the salad and add the raspberry vinegar. Add the croutons and toss. Correct the seasoning.

NOTE: The croutons can be made up to 1 day in advance and kept in an airtight plastic bag once cooled.

SERVES 6 TO 8

CHEF'S TIP

Raspberry vinegar can be made at home with fresh or dry-pack frozen raspberries. Bring white distilled vinegar to a boil, add the fruit and allow it to mellow for at least 3 days.

GOAT CHEESE IN PHYLLO

ANDRÉ POIROT, NEW ORLEANS, LOUISIANA

Phyllo dough is used in Italian cooking as well as in Greek and Middle Eastern. This is served as an appetizer, but it could also be a light lunch dish.

6 ounces fresh goat cheese
2 teaspoons cracked black pepper
¼ cup herbes de Provence or Italian seasoning
12 sheets phyllo dough (for handling, see pages 25–26)
¾ cup virgin olive oil
4 tomatoes, sliced ¼ inch thick
4 zucchini, sliced ¼ inch thick
4 yellow squash, sliced ¼ inch thick
Salt
2 cups shredded lettuce

Cut the cheese into 12 medallions and sprinkle them with a little cracked black pepper and herb seasoning. Brush each sheet of phyllo dough with olive oil, and cut into 3 equal pieces vertically. Stack the 3 sections on top of each other. Place 1 medallion of goat cheese in the top corner and fold into a triangle.

Preheat the oven to 400°F. Place the tomato, zucchini, and yellow squash slices on a baking sheet, brush them with ¼ cup of the olive oil, and season with salt, pepper, and mixed herb seasoning. Bake for 5 to 6 minutes, or until tender. Meanwhile, in a medium sauté pan or skillet, heat the remaining olive oil over medium heat and cook the phyllo packets until browned on both sides, about 3 to 4 minutes. Arrange the vegetables around the edge of a heated plate and put the lettuce in the center of the plate. Place the phyllo packets atop the bed of lettuce.

NOTE: The packets can be prepared 1 day in advance and refrigerated with sheets of wax paper between the layers. Bake the vegetables and sauté the phyllo packets just prior to serving.

SERVES 4

GRILLED GOAT CHEESE WITH SUN-DRIED TOMATOES

Jeremiah Tower, San Francisco, California

Goat cheese and sun-dried tomatoes are two ingredients that reflect the Italian influence on New American Cuisine. In this easy appetizer—perfect for a summer dinner—the two are joined and the flavors blend beautifully.

4 ounces fresh white goat cheese
8 pieces sun-dried tomatoes packed in olive oil
1/2 cup olive oil
8 grape leaves, either fresh or packed in brine and rinsed well
16 slices Italian bread, each 1/4 inch thick
Salt and freshly ground black pepper

Light a gas or charcoal grill. Cut the goat cheese into 4 slices, and set aside. Gently pound the tomatoes until flat with the flat side of a meat mallet. Dip rounds of goat cheese in olive oil, then place a flattened tomato on the top and bottom of each round. Remove the stems from the grape leaves, and wrap the cheese and tomatoes in grape leaves (1 or 2 grape leaves should cover).

Brush the bread with some of the remaining olive oil and sprinkle with salt and pepper to taste. Grill the bread for 20 to 30 seconds per side, or until toasted, turning the bread gently with tongs. Drip olive oil on the grape leaves, then grill the packets 5 minutes on each side. Serve at once, using the croutons to scoop out the melted cheese.

NOTE: The cheese packets can be prepared up to 1 day in advance and refrigerated, and the toast can be broiled at the same time. Do not grill the cheese until just before serving.

Serves 4

TOMATO TARTS

KEIL MOSHIER, NEW ORLEANS, LOUISIANA

These little individual tarts are wonderful appetizers, or can be a casual lunch if served with a salad. If you use purchased pie crust sheets, either cut them out individually or make two and cut them into quarters before serving.

CRUST
3 cups all-purpose flour
Pinch of salt
Pinch of sugar
1 cup (2 sticks) cold unsalted butter
$^1/_2$ cup vegetable shortening
5 to 6 tablespoons cold water

TOPPING
1 cup chopped plum tomatoes
$^1/_2$ cup minced fresh basil leaves
$^1/_4$ cup minced fresh thyme
1 cup crumbled goat, feta, or shredded mozzarella cheese
Sliced plum tomatoes and black olives, for garnish
8 teaspoons olive oil

To make the crust, combine the flour, salt, and sugar. With a pastry cutter or your fingers, cut in the butter and shortening until the mixture resembles oatmeal. Add cold water and mix until all the ingredients are moistened. Form into a ball. Cover and chill for 30 minutes.

Preheat the oven to 375°F. On a lightly floured surface, roll out the dough $^1/_8$ inch thick. Cut into eight 3-inch rounds with a cookie cutter or an inverted glass. Prick the dough all over with a fork. Place on a baking sheet and bake until the dough is tan.

Top the dough with the chopped tomatoes, basil, thyme, and cheese, and garnish with sliced tomatoes and black olives. Drizzle each tart with a little olive oil. Bake for 4 to 5 minutes, or until the cheese has melted. Serve immediately.

NOTE: The crusts can be baked up to 1 day in advance and kept at room temperature. Bake the tarts just prior to serving.

SERVES 8

FRIED CALAMARI

GOFFREDO FRACCARO, NEW ORLEANS, LOUISIANA

Fried calamari are a great treat, and if the oil is sufficiently hot they are tender and juicy. Most squid is sold already cleaned, and all that is needed is to cut it apart; however, directions are given below "just in case."

1 dozen squid
4 cups vegetable oil
1 cup all-purpose flour
Salt and freshly ground black pepper
2 lemons, cut into wedges

To clean the squid, remove the head, tentacles, and arms. Remove all material from the body cavity, including the cartilage and the ink sac. Discard all except the ink sac, if you want to use it. Peel off the skin, and rinse the squid meat thoroughly, inside and out, under cool running water. Rinse the body and the tentacles thoroughly, inside and out. The squid should be creamy white, with possibly a little purple on the edges.

Cut into pieces and rinse in cold water. Heat the vegetable oil to 385°F. Drain the squid well, pat dry on paper towels, and dredge in flour, shaking off the excess. Carefully fry in hot oil until golden brown. Do not crowd the pot; it is better to fry in batches, if necessary. Season with salt and pepper and serve immediately, with the lemon wedges.

NOTE: The squid can be prepared for dredging up to 1 day in advance and refrigerated, tightly covered. Do not fry them until just prior to serving.

SERVES 8 TO 10 AS AN APPETIZER, 6 AS AN ENTRÉE

CALAMARI WITH SPINACH

FERNANDO SARACCHI, NEW ORLEANS, LOUISIANA

Grilled Polenta (page 168) triangles are the base for the topping of spinach and spicy baby squid. Squid may be purchased frozen, but it is infinitely better fresh.

3 tablespoons extra-virgin olive oil
2 garlic cloves, peeled and minced
6 ounces cleaned baby squid
Salt and freshly ground black pepper
Pinch of dried red pepper flakes
$\frac{1}{3}$ cup dry white wine
2 tablespoons unsalted butter
$\frac{1}{4}$ pound spinach leaves, washed and stemmed

Heat the olive oil in a medium sauté pan over medium heat. Sauté the garlic until golden, about 1 minute. Remove the garlic from the pan with a slotted spoon. Season the squid with salt, black pepper, and red pepper flakes, and sauté it on both sides for 3 to 4 minutes, or until crisp. Add the wine and cook until the wine has evaporated, about 4 minutes. Add 1 tablespoon butter and mix it in.

In another medium sauté pan or skillet, melt the remaining 1 tablespoon butter over medium heat. Add the spinach leaves and sauté until wilted, about 2 minutes.

To serve, place 1 triangle of polenta on each of 4 plates. Top each serving with an equal amount of wilted spinach and calamari.

SERVES 4

CHEF'S TIP

Buy squid that have been cleaned, but make sure the purplish skin is pulled off and discarded. Check to see that the quill (a small, thick, plasticlike blade) is removed from the body. Rinse the squid under cold water to remove any sand, and pat dry. If your guests are squeamish about tentacles, chop them finely and add to the pan. Squid should have a sweet, mild flavor and no fishy smell. They are high in protein, extremely low in fat, and very inexpensive.

MARINATED OYSTERS

Gerhard Brill, Orange Beach, Alabama

This dish can be served as part of a buffet, or just with the oysters topping some crusty Italian bread. It is incredibly easy to make and lighter than most cooked oyster dishes.

24 oysters, shucked (pages 17–18)
¹/₄ cup oyster water (juice from the oysters plus water to make
   ¹/₄ cup)
¹/₂ cup shallots, minced
¹/₄ cup chopped parsley
¹/₂ cup white wine
¹/₄ teaspoon black pepper
4 tablespoons (¹/₂ stick) unsalted butter, softened
3 tablespoons all-purpose flour
Salt and freshly ground black pepper

In a shallow pan, poach the oysters in the oyster water with the shallots, parsley, wine, and black pepper. Bring to a boil and cook 1 minute. Blend the butter with the flour. Stir the butter/flour mixture gently into the oysters until thoroughly blended and thickened, about 30 seconds. Adjust the seasonings before serving.

Note: This dish must be prepared just prior to serving.

Serves 6

OYSTERS GABIE

GREG SONNIER, NEW ORLEANS, LOUISIANA

Seasoned bread crumbs are always a great topping for baked seafood. Delicate artichokes and hearty pancetta are the ingredients that enliven this dish, which can be served with Hollandaise Sauce (pages 15–16), should one want it richer.

1 lemon, halved
¼ cup olive oil
2 large artichokes, trimmed (page 8)
4 ounces pancetta, finely diced
1 tablespoon butter
¼ cup chopped green onions (white part only), or shallots
1 tablespoon minced garlic
2 tablespoons minced fresh parsley
Juice of 1 lemon
Salt and freshly ground black pepper
¼ cup plus 2 tablespoons dry bread crumbs
¼ cup plus 2 tablespoons grated Parmesan cheese
15 to 20 large plump oysters, drained, with liquor reserved

LIDIA BASTIANICH
CHEF AND OWNER, FELIDIA, NEW YORK, NY

Why did you become a chef?
I come from a family of cooks, as does my husband. While in school I worked in restaurants and decided I really enjoyed cooking.

How did you receive your training?
I started getting hands-on experience at the age of sixteen, and had my first restaurant at the age of twenty-two. I've gone back to Italy to study informally, working alongside top chefs.

Any tips to pass on?
Home cooks should understand ingredients, since 50 percent of the final product is the quality of the ingredients. Sometimes less is better with spices and similar ingredients; build a reference library in your mind of spices and their flavors.

Place the halved lemon and 2 tablespoons of the olive oil in a large pot of boiling water. Add the artichokes and cook until tender, about 20 minutes. Drain and cool. Pull off the leaves and scrape off the pulp at their bases. Discard the leaves. Dig out the choke with a spoon and dice the remaining heart. Set aside with the scraped pulp.

Preheat the oven to 450°F. In a medium sauté pan or skillet, heat 1 tablespoon of the olive oil and cook the pancetta until brown; add the remaining tablespoon of oil and the butter. Sauté the green onions or shallots, garlic, and parsley until tender, 3 to 4 minutes. Add the diced artichokes and lemon juice. If the dressing looks too dry, add a little oyster liquor to moisten. Sauté for about 2 minutes. Add salt and pepper to taste. Remove from heat, add $1/4$ cup of the bread crumbs and $1/4$ cup of the Parmesan cheese, and toss lightly.

Place 4 to 5 oysters into each of 4 individual ovenproof casseroles. Top with the artichoke dressing. Sprinkle with the remaining 2 tablespoons cheese and 2 tablespoons bread crumbs. Bake until browned, 10 to 15 minutes.

NOTE: The casseroles can be prepared up to 2 hours in advance of baking.

SERVES 4

CHEF'S TIP

Save and freeze any leftover oyster liquor to add to fish stocks.

OYSTERS WITH GARLIC BUTTER

WARREN LE RUTH, BAY ST. LOUIS, MISSISSIPPI

All you need to embellish this appetizer is a lot of crusty bread to sop up the luscious garlicky butter sauce topping the oysters. Add a few oysters and a tossed salad, and you have a great lunch.

2 cups (1 pound) unsalted butter, softened
1 teaspoon salt
1 teaspoon freshly ground white pepper
$^1/_3$ cup olive oil
$^1/_4$ cup white wine
$^1/_4$ cup chopped fresh parsley
$^1/_4$ cup finely chopped onion
6 garlic cloves, peeled and finely chopped
3 dozen oysters, shucked (pages 17–18)

Preheat the oven to 400°F. Whip the butter with an electric mixer until smooth. Add the salt, white pepper, olive oil, and wine to the butter and blend. Add the parsley, onion, and garlic and mix on high speed, scraping down the sides occasionally, until the butter turns white, about 5 to 7 minutes.

Place 6 oysters in each of 6 gratin dishes, and top with the garlic butter. Bake for 10 minutes, or until the edges of the oysters have curled. Serve immediately.

NOTE: The butter can be prepared up to 2 days in advance and refrigerated, tightly covered. Allow it to reach room temperature and soften before topping the oysters.

SERVES 6

OYSTERS IN GARLIC AND MUSHROOM BUTTER

Roland Huet, New Orleans, Louisiana

The combination of butter, garlic, and parsley is a classic in both Italian and French cuisines. In this case, they top tender oysters. Serve a lot of bread with this dish to enjoy the sauce.

³/₄ **pound fresh mushrooms**
2 garlic cloves, peeled and minced
1 bunch parsley
1¹/₂ cups (3 sticks) unsalted butter, softened
1 cup bread crumbs
¹/₄ teaspoon nutmeg
Salt and freshly ground black pepper
3 dozen oysters

Pulse mushrooms, garlic, and parsley in a food processor until finely chopped. Add the butter and pulse again until blended well. Add the bread crumbs, nutmeg, salt, and pepper. Reserve.

Poach the oysters in their own juices until they are just simmering and the edges begin to curl. Cool in the juices to prevent drying, then drain on a cloth.

Preheat the broiler. Place 6 oysters each in of six 4¹/₂-inch gratin dishes. Smooth the mushroom/butter mixture over the oysters and place under the broiler until brown and bubbly. Serve immediately.

NOTE: The oysters can be poached up to 1 day in advance and kept refrigerated. Broil them just prior to serving.

SERVES 6

CROSTINI WITH CHICKEN LIVERS

ADRIANA GIRAMONTI, MILL VALLEY, CALIFORNIA

These flavorful chicken liver toasts can be served as an appetizer, along with a salad, as a light luncheon, or they can be passed as hors d'oeuvre for a cocktail party.

2 tablespoons unsalted butter
2 tablespoons olive oil
1 small onion, peeled and chopped
1 garlic clove, crushed
$1/2$ pound chicken livers, chopped very fine
$1/2$ cup white wine
Salt and freshly ground black pepper
2 teaspoons minced parsley
$1/4$ cup heavy cream
$1/2$ cup demi-glace (pages 12–13)
18 slices day-old Italian bread, cut $1/4$ inch thick

In a sauté pan, heat 1 tablespoon of the butter and all the olive oil over medium heat. Add the onion and garlic. Sauté lightly until the onion is translucent. Add the chopped livers and sauté well over high heat for about 3 minutes or less. Add the white wine, salt, pepper, and parsley. As soon as the wine has evaporated, add the cream, remaining 1 tablespoon butter, and demi-glace. Simmer on low heat for about 1 minute.

Preheat the oven to 400°F. Place the bread slices on a baking pan in the oven for 2 to 3 minutes, or until lightly toasted. Spread the liver mixture on the toasted bread to serve.

NOTE: The chicken liver mixture can be made up to 3 hours in advance and kept at room temperature, and the toasts can be made at the same time. Reheat the chicken livers over low heat, stirring gently.

SERVES 6

LIVER MOUSSE WITH TOMATO SAUCE

UDO NECHUTNYS, ST. HELENA, CALIFORNIA

Using poultry livers is part of the Italian tradition, and this mousse, served with a rich tomato sauce, is made in minutes in the food processor.

$^1/_2$ onion, peeled and sliced
1 pound chicken livers
2 shallots, peeled and halved
1 sprig fresh thyme
2 garlic cloves, peeled
2 sprigs fresh parsley
2 sprigs fresh basil
3 eggs
$^1/_4$ pound duck fat or vegetable shortening, melted
1 cup bread crumbs
1 cup heavy cream
Salt and freshly ground black pepper
Tomato Sauce (page 174)

Preheat the oven to 450°F. Grease eight 6-ounce ovenproof ramekins and place them in a roasting pan. Bring a large kettle of water to a boil.

Place all the ingredients except the tomato sauce in a food processor fitted with the steel blade and purée until smooth. Ladle the mixture into the prepared ramekins, cover the cups with buttered parchment paper or aluminum foil, and place the roasting pan in the oven. Pour boiling water halfway up the sides of the pan, and bake the ramekins for 10 to 12 minutes, or until a knife inserted in the center comes out clean. Remove the pan from the oven, and allow the mousse to sit in the hot water for 5 minutes.

To serve, invert the ramekins onto serving plates, and spoon the tomato sauce around them.

NOTE: The mousse can be prepared for baking up to a few hours in advance and kept at room temperature. Bake just prior to serving.

SERVES 8

VEAL SAUSAGE

MICHAEL FOLEY, CHICAGO, ILLINOIS

The New American twist on a classic Italian fennel-scented sausage is the use of bourbon as a flavoring agent. These make a wonderful appetizer, and can be served with Tomato Sauce (page 174) or alone. Note that this recipe must be started two days ahead.

1 pound veal, cut in 1-inch cubes
1 pound fatback, cut in 1-inch cubes
2 teaspoons salt
6 peppercorns, crushed
2 teaspoons freshly ground black pepper
$\frac{1}{2}$ medium onion, finely chopped
3 tablespoons fennel seed
2 garlic cloves, peeled and minced
$\frac{1}{4}$ cup clarified butter (page 11)
$\frac{1}{3}$ cup bourbon
Pork casings

Combine the veal and fatback, and pass through a meat grinder or chop coarsely in a food processor using on and off pulsing action. Add the salt, crushed peppercorns, and freshly ground pepper.

Sauté the chopped onion, fennel, and chopped garlic in half the clarified butter (2 tablespoons) until the onions become translucent. Remove the onion mixture from the heat; drain and cool. Pour the bourbon over the ground veal and fatback; then add the cooled onion mixture. Marinate in the refrigerator for 2 days; then stuff into the casings to make sausages.

Poach the sausages in simmering water for 10 minutes. Drain and dry; cook over medium heat in the remaining 2 tablespoons clarified butter until brown.

NOTE: The sausages can be frozen for up to 3 months before cooking. The sausage mixture can also be formed into balls as hors d'oeuvre and baked for 20 minutes at 375°F. Any sausage mixture can be formed into patties and cooked without casings by sautéing the patties over medium heat until browned.

SERVES 8 AS AN APPETIZER, 4 AS AN ENTRÉE

CARPACCIO OF SIRLOIN

SETH RAYNOR, NANTUCKET, MASSACHUSETTS

Unlike the classic Italian carpaccio that is merely drizzled with oil and served with cheese, this American version adds lusty garlicky aioli with three different flavorings to the mix. This easy dish looks as good as it tastes.

4 slices of beef sirloin (2 ounces each), sliced 1/4 inch thick
1 egg
1 egg yolk
1 tablespoon plus 1 teaspoon water
6 garlic cloves
1 1/2 cups olive oil
Juice of 1/2 lemon
1 tablespoon Dijon mustard
3 fresh basil leaves, cut into a chiffonade (page 15)

Place the sirloin slices between 2 sheets of plastic wrap. Using the dull side of a meat pounder or the bottom of a heavy pan, pound the meat until it is paper-thin. Remove the plastic wrap and check for and remove any fat or gristle that may remain. Refrigerate the beef, putting plastic wrap between the slices.

To make the sauce, put the whole egg and the egg yolk in a blender or food processor and combine. Add 1 tablespoon of water and the garlic and purée for 30 seconds. With the motor running, add the olive oil a few drops at a time at the beginning, then gradually in a thin stream. Add the lemon juice and pulse to combine. The mixture should now be a light, garlicky mayonnaise. Add the remaining water if necessary.

Divide the sauce between 2 bowls. Add the Dijon mustard to one bowl of mayonnaise, and stir until well blended. Stir the basil chiffonade into the other bowl, and set aside.

To assemble, place a slice of sirloin in the center of each plate. Spoon a tablespoon of each sauce around the outside of the carpaccio.

NOTE: The meat and sauces can be prepared 6 hours in advance and refrigerated, tightly covered.

SERVES 4

PORCINI BROTH WITH SOFT POLENTA

Jody Adams, Cambridge, Massachusetts

This is one of the most comforting dishes imaginable, with creamy polenta and aromatic broth as foils to poached eggs. Service it with a tossed salad and some crusty bread, perhaps with a second egg, to make this a casual supper.

Porcini Stock
2 tablespoons dried porcini mushrooms
3½ cups chicken stock
½ cup dry marsala wine
Salt and freshly ground black pepper

Poached Eggs
1 tablespoon vinegar
Pinch of salt
4 extra-large eggs

Creamy Polenta (page 169)
Four 1-ounce slices taleggio or fontina cheese
Truffle oil or extra-virgin olive oil

To make the stock, soak the porcini mushrooms in just enough water to cover for 1 hour. Strain the liquid through a fine mesh sieve, reserving the soaking water. Combine the mushroom water, chicken stock, and marsala in a medium saucepan. Chop the soaked mushrooms, add them to the pan, and bring the stock to a boil over medium-high heat. Reduce the heat and simmer for 45 minutes. Season with salt and pepper. Strain the mushrooms and reserve the broth.

To make the poached eggs, fill a shallow 8-inch sauté pan or skillet with water. Bring the water to a boil over high heat, then reduce to a simmer. Add the vinegar and salt. Crack the eggs, one at a time, into a cup, and slide them into the simmering water. Poach the eggs for 3 to 4 minutes. Remove the cooked eggs gently from the pan with a slotted spoon. Transfer the eggs to a bowl of ice water and reserve until needed.

Preheat the oven to 350°F. Spoon ¹/₂ cup polenta into each of 4 low ovenproof soup bowls. Press a slice of the taleggio cheese into the polenta. Bake in the preheated oven until the cheese begins to melt into the polenta, about 4 minutes. While the polenta is baking, reheat the porcini stock.

Reheat the poached eggs in the hot broth. Remove the eggs with a slotted spoon and place on top of the cheese and polenta. Pour the broth into the soup bowls and drizzle the truffle oil or extra-virgin olive oil over the broth.

NOTE: The broth can be made up to 3 days in advance and refrigerated, tightly covered. The polenta can be prepared and the eggs can be poached 1 day in advance.

SERVES 4

CREAM OF GARLIC SOUP

DANIEL BONNOT, NEW ORLEANS, LOUISIANA

Not only is garlic soup part of the Italian tradition, so is thickening soups with stale bread. In this version, the soup is creamed, but the cream could be replaced with additional chicken stock for a lighter version.

4 tablespoons ('/₂ stick) unsalted butter
2 onions, peeled and thinly sliced
4 heads garlic, cloves peeled and mashed
1 quart chicken stock
¹/₂ pound day-old French bread
1 bay leaf
2 sprigs fresh thyme
³/₄ cup heavy cream
Salt and freshly ground black pepper

Melt the butter in a soup kettle and add the onion and garlic. Cook for 5 minutes over moderate heat. Add the stock, and simmer for 10 minutes. Stir in the bread slices and add the bay leaf and thyme.

Simmer for 10 minutes longer, discard the bay leaf and thyme, and purée the soup in a blender or food processor. Return it to the soup pot, add the cream, and bring to a simmer. Season with salt and pepper to taste, and serve.

NOTE: The soup can be prepared up to 2 days in advance and refrigerated, tightly covered. Reheat over low heat.

SERVES 4

CHEF'S TIP

Any soup made with starchy ingredients like bread or potatoes may thicken when chilled. Thin to a more desirable consistency with milk, cream, or stock while reheating.

KALE SOUP

EMERIL LAGASSE, NEW ORLEANS, LOUISIANA

This is a very easy soup to make for a crowd, and it is hearty and delicious. To make it into a meal with a tossed salad and garlic bread, add a few cans of white beans to the soup.

1 pound garlic pork sausage
1 tablespoon olive oil
1 large onion, peeled and diced
4 garlic cloves, peeled and minced
$1/2$ red bell pepper, diced
Salt and freshly ground black pepper
3 quarts chicken stock
5 bay leaves
1 head kale, washed, stemmed, and roughly chopped
2 large baking potatoes, peeled and diced
$1/4$ teaspoon crushed dried red pepper

Slice the sausage and sauté over medium heat in the olive oil in a stockpot. When the sausage is cooked halfway, add the onion, garlic, and red bell pepper. Season with salt and pepper. Cook until the vegetables are translucent, then pour in the chicken stock. Heat the mixture to the boiling point and add the bay leaves and kale. When the soup returns to a boil, stir in the potatoes and the crushed dried red pepper. Simmer for 45 minutes to 1 hour, discard the bay leaves, and season with salt and pepper. Serve immediately.

NOTE: The soup is better if made 1 day in advance and reheated; it brings out the different flavors.

SERVES 10 TO 12

PERFECT PASTAS AND ROBUST RICE

Even twenty years ago, pasta meant boxes of either
spaghetti or perhaps lasagne in the minds of most
Americans. But those days are gone forever as chefs
and home cooks alike explore the myriad of shapes,
textures, and flavors of both dried and fresh pasta.
For a few years the pendulum swung too far the other
way, and cooks were abandoning toothsome dried
pasta entirely, thinking fresh was always better. That
is not the case. Dried pastas should be used with
heartier dishes; fresh pastas match with subtler dishes.
While many of the recipes in this chapter call for
making your own pasta dough, do not bypass a
recipe for that reason. Buy the fresh pasta
at the market, and enjoy the sauce.

BUTTERNUT SQUASH RAVIOLI WITH CREAM AND ASIAGO CHEESE

JOHN DRAZ, WINNETKA, ILLINOIS

This is an elegant vegetarian pasta with a colorful filling; it is simply sauced with reduced cream.

RAVIOLI
1 medium butternut squash
Pinch of nutmeg
Salt and freshly ground white pepper
Basic Pasta Dough (page 22)
1 egg, beaten

SAUCE
2¹/₂ cups heavy cream
¹/₂ cup grated Asiago cheese
Salt and white pepper

JOHANNE KILLEEN AND GEORGE GERMON
CHEF AND OWNERS, AL FORNO, PROVIDENCE, RI

Why did you become a chef?
Our becoming chefs was never a conscious decision; it just happened. We were both trained as artists and were working in our respective freelance projects when we started working together in a restaurant kitchen as a sideline. Our relationship began and flourished and we decided to open a small business together.

How did you receive your training?
We are both self-taught, and travel extensively.

Any tips to pass on?
You can only cook well if your kitchen is clean.

To make the filling, pare and seed the squash. Dice into small cubes and place in a steamer set over 2 inches of boiling water. Steam until tender, about 10 to 12 minutes. Place the steamed squash in a food processor and purée. Season with nutmeg, salt, and white pepper. Remove from the processor and cool.

Make the pasta dough and roll into 6 evenly trimmed, 12-inch-long sheets of pasta. On a floured board, brush one sheet of pasta with the beaten egg. Place 4 spoonfuls of squash ½ inch from the near edge, about 1 inch apart, along the length of the pasta sheet. Fold the far edge of the pasta over the filling so that it meets the near edge. Lightly press the top and bottom layers between the pockets of filling to force out any excess air. Using a fluted ravioli wheel, cut and seal the ravioli by running the wheel between the pockets and along the sides. Repeat with the remaining pasta sheets.

To make the sauce, in a shallow pan, simmer the cream and reduce to two-thirds the volume. Stir in the grated cheese and simmer to melt. Adjust the seasoning and reserve, keeping warm.

To serve, bring a large pot of salted water to a boil. Plunge the ravioli into the water. Cook al dente, about 2 minutes. Remove the ravioli from the pot with a slotted spoon and toss them gently in the sauce until well coated. Garnish with more cheese.

NOTE: The ravioli can be prepared up to 2 days in advance and refrigerated, tossed with cornmeal and with sheets of wax paper separating the layers.

SERVES 4

CHEF'S TIP

Acorn squash and butternut squash have almost identical flavors, and can be substituted for one another in any recipe.

FETTUCCINE ALLA GOFFREDO

GOFFREDO FRACCARO, NEW ORLEANS, LOUISIANA

Pasta dishes don't get any easier than this one, or any more delicious. To make this a whole meal, add some leftover roast chicken or fish to the pasta, and serve a tossed salad.

Basic Pasta Dough (page 22)
¹/₂ cup (1 stick) butter, melted
¹/₂ cup heavy cream
1 cup grated Parmesan cheese
Salt and freshly ground white pepper

Bring a large pot of salted water to a boil. Cut the pasta dough into thin ribbons for fettuccine. Cook the pasta al dente, and drain.

Heat the butter and cream in a large, deep-sided pan; do not boil. Add the fettuccine noodles and toss. Add the cheese and mix with a fork and spoon until all the ingredients are well blended and a creamy sauce forms. Season with salt and pepper, and serve.

NOTE: The raw pasta can be made 1 day in advance.

SERVES 4

CHEF'S TIP

Always add Parmesan cheese to a recipe before tasting for salt, since the cheese contains some salt.

SHRIMP WITH FETTUCCINE

GERHARD BRILL, ORANGE BEACH, ALABAMA

This is one of those elegant dishes that is very quick to make, especially if the shrimp are purchased already shelled and deveined. The sauce is made in about the same amount of time it takes the water to come to a boil. If pasta sticks together when cooked, plunge it back into boiling water for 45 seconds and it will separate.

1/4 pound (1 stick) unsalted butter
2 garlic cloves, peeled and minced
4 medium white onions, peeled and thinly sliced
4 large mushrooms, thinly sliced
1/2 cup coarsely chopped scallions
1/4 cup peeled, seeded, and chopped fresh tomatoes (page 30)
1 tablespoon minced parsley
1 pound raw shrimp, peeled and deveined
1/4 teaspoon dried oregano
1/4 teaspoon dried thyme
1/4 cup shrimp stock or bottled clam juice
1/4 cup white wine
Salt and freshly ground black pepper
3/4 pound fresh fettuccine

Bring a large pot of salted water to a boil. Place half the butter (1/2 stick) in a sauté pan over medium heat. Add the garlic, onions, mushrooms, and scallions, and sauté for 3 minutes. Add the tomatoes, parsley, shrimp, oregano, thyme, stock, and wine. Cook over high heat for 3 minutes, or until the shrimp are pink and the liquid is slightly reduced. Season with salt and pepper to taste. Remove from the heat and set aside.

Cook the fettuccine until al dente, and drain well. To serve, swirl the remaining 1/2 stick butter into the shrimp, and toss with the pasta.

NOTE: The sauce, up to adding the butter, can be prepared up to 3 hours in advance and kept at room temperature. Cook the pasta and add the butter just prior to serving.

SERVES 4

CRABMEAT RAVIOLI

GOFFREDO FRACCARO, NEW ORLEANS, LOUISIANA

Crabmeat is very delicate and sweet, and this recipe allows the taste to shine. Serve it with a green salad, and some crusty bread for a main course.

Basic Pasta Dough (page 22)

RAVIOLI
3 tablespoons unsalted butter
2 tablespoons all-purpose flour
1¼ cups heavy cream, heated
Salt and freshly ground white pepper
1 pound lump crabmeat, picked over for shells
¼ cup minced green onions
½ cup cracker crumbs

SAUCE
½ cup heavy cream
4 tablespoons (½ stick) unsalted butter, softened
¼ cup freshly grated Parmesan cheese
Salt and freshly ground white pepper

Prepare the pasta dough, wrap it in plastic wrap, and let it rest.

For the ravioli, melt 2 tablespoons of the butter over low heat in a medium saucepan, and add the flour. Cook for 2 or 3 minutes, whisking all the time. Add the heated cream gradually, whisking to avoid lumps, until the sauce thickens. Let the mixture simmer until reduced to 1 cup, then season with salt and pepper. Set aside to cool.

Add the crabmeat to the cooled sauce. Melt the remaining 1 tablespoon butter in a small skillet and sauté the onions for 3 minutes, or until they are translucent. Add the green onions and cracker crumbs to the sauce, mix well, and chill. Form into balls the size of a large marble.

Roll the pasta dough into very thin sheets through a pasta maker or with a rolling pin. Place the crabmeat balls about 1½ inches apart on the long side of a sheet of the pasta dough. Paint the area between the balls with water and top with a second sheet of dough. Form ravioli by pressing around each ball to form a seal. Dust with flour and cut into squares with a fluted ravioli wheel.

To make the sauce, bring the cream to a boil in a small saucepan and simmer until reduced by one-third. Add the butter, stir in the cheese, and season with salt and pepper.

Bring a large pot of salted water to a boil. Cook the ravioli for 5 minutes in rapidly boiling salted water. Drain carefully, and gently toss with the sauce. Serve immediately.

NOTE: The ravioli can be prepared up to 1 day in advance and refrigerated, with layers of wax paper between layers of ravioli. Cook and sauce just prior to serving.

SERVES 4 TO 6

CHEF'S TIP

Ravioli can always be cut apart with a pizza wheel or a knife and fork if a ravioli cutter is not available.

LINGUINE WITH SEAFOOD

ADRIANA GIRAMONTI, MILL VALLEY, CALIFORNIA

An easy way to peel garlic is to place the cloves on their sides on a cutting board and press on them with the side of a chef's knife. This will break the skin, which will then peel right off.

1 pound dry linguine
All-purpose flour for dredging
1 pound medium prawns, cleaned and deveined
1 pound fresh salmon fillet, coarsely julienned
¹/₂ cup olive oil
1 cup leeks, cleaned and julienned (page 16)
2 cups sliced mushrooms
¹/₂ cup white wine
1 tablespoon marjoram
1 tablespoon minced fresh parsley
2 garlic cloves, peeled and minced
Salt and freshly ground black pepper
2 tablespoons unsalted butter
1 cup chicken or fish stock (bottled clam juice may be substituted)

Boil the linguine according to package instructions. Cool under cold running water, drain well, and reserve.

Flour the prawns and salmon lightly. In a large sauté pan, heat the olive oil over high heat, then add the prawns and salmon and sauté for 1 to 2 minutes, or until the prawns are pink. Remove from the pan with a slotted spoon, and set aside.

Add the leeks to the pan and sauté 1 minute, then add the mushrooms and sauté for 1 minute more. Add the wine, marjoram, parsley, garlic, salt, pepper, and butter. Sauté lightly. Add the stock, lower the heat, and simmer for 2 minutes, adding more stock if the mixture becomes too dry. Add drained linguine, shrimp, and salmon and mix well. Simmer for 1 minute, and serve.

NOTE: This dish should be made just prior to serving; however the vegetables and fish can be prepared for cooking a few hours in advance and refrigerated.

SERVES 6

TWO-SALMON PASTA

KATHY RUIZ, HOUSTON, TEXAS

10 ounces smoked salmon
10 ounces fresh salmon fillet
1 cup fish stock
2 tablespoons clarified butter (page 11)
3/4 cup peeled, seeded, and chopped tomatoes (page 30)
1/4 cup chopped shallots
1 1/2 teaspoons minced garlic
4 teaspoons chopped fresh dill
1 teaspoon chopped fresh rosemary
Salt and freshly ground white pepper
1/2 cup heavy cream
6 green onions, white part only, chopped
Basic Pasta Dough (page 22), cut into fettuccine

GARNISHES
Sour cream
Caviar

Flake the smoked salmon and set aside. Poach the fresh salmon fillet in the fish stock until cooked, about 5 minutes. Remove from the stock, reserving the stock, and then flake the salmon. Set aside.

Heat the butter in a large, deep sauté pan or skillet and add the tomatoes, shallots, and garlic. Sauté for 2 minutes, then add the dill and rosemary. Season with salt and white pepper, then add the reserved fish stock and cream. Reduce the sauce by half, or until it reaches a syrupy consistency. Then stir in the green onions and both kinds of salmon.

Cook the pasta in boiling water until just al dente, about 1 minute. Drain.

To serve, toss the pasta with the sauce, and top with a dollop of sour cream and some caviar.

NOTE: The pasta can be made a few days in advance and allowed to dry (increase the cooking time if dried). The sauce can be prepared in advance to the point of adding the fish and green onions. Reheat gently to a simmer and then add the final ingredients.

SERVES 6

TORTELLINI

ANDREA APUZZO, NEW ORLEANS, LOUISIANA

Filled with meats and cheeses and simply sauced with butter, Parmesan, and sage, tortellini are among the most famous authentically Italian pasta dishes. The tortellini are also delicious served in a simple chicken broth.

1/2 pound ground veal
1/2 pound ground beef
2 carrots, peeled and finely diced
1 small onion, peeled and finely diced
2 stalks celery, finely diced
1 teaspoon tomato paste
1 tablespoon ricotta cheese
1/2 pound mozzarella cheese, shredded
Pinch of ground nutmeg
Pinch of dried oregano
1 teaspoon chopped fresh basil
Basic Pasta Dough (page 22)
1 egg, lightly beaten
1 tablespoon olive oil
1/4 teaspoon salt
4 tablespoons (1/2 stick) unsalted butter
1/2 cup grated Parmesan cheese
1 tablespoon chopped fresh sage
Salt and freshly ground black pepper

To make the filling, place the veal, beef, carrots, onion, celery, tomato paste, ricotta, mozzarella, nutmeg, oregano, and basil in a food processor fitted with the steel blade. Pulse the machine just until the mixture is thoroughly combined. Set aside while rolling the pasta.

Roll the pasta as thinly as possible. Cut into $2^{3}/_{4}$-inch rounds with a circular cookie or biscuit cutter. Brush the rounds with egg wash and place a scant teaspoon of filling on the center of each. Fold the circles in half and press the edges together to seal. Form into cap shapes by first stretching the stuffed pasta around your finger like a ring. Press the ends together, flipping the edges up like a hat brim. Place the tortellini on a tray dusted with flour.

Cook the tortellini in boiling water to which 1 tablespoon olive oil and 1 teaspoon salt have been added. Boil for 8 to 10 minutes, stirring occasionally, until tender. Drain, reserving $^{1}/_{4}$ cup of the water.

Melt the butter in a sauté pan. Add the tortellini, Parmesan, fresh sage, and $^{1}/_{4}$ cup of the pasta cooking water. Season with salt and pepper, toss, and serve.

NOTE: The tortellini can be made up to 2 days in advance and refrigerated with layers of wax paper between the layers; any leftover filling can be frozen for future use.

SERVES 8

CHEESE PASTA ROLL WITH TOMATO SAUCE

WERNER ALBRECHT, SAN FRANCISCO, CALIFORNIA

This is a beautiful dish, with swirls of white cheese and pink meats in a green pasta. It is excellent for a buffet dinner, since it does not need a knife, and can be eaten at room temperature.

2 tablespoons unsalted butter
$^1/_2$ cup diced smoked ham
4 scallions, minced
1 package (8 ounces) cream cheese, softened
$^1/_4$ cup grated Parmesan cheese
$^1/_2$ cup ricotta cheese
$^1/_2$ teaspoon freshly ground black pepper
2 eggs
2 sheets of fresh spinach pasta, 12 × 4 inches each (pages 22–25)
Melted butter
$^1/_2$ pound prosciutto, very thinly sliced
1 gallon chicken stock
Tomato Sauce (page 174)
Chopped chives, for garnish

In a sauté pan, melt the butter and add the diced ham and scallions. Cook over medium heat about 2 minutes, until the scallions are soft. Beat the cream cheese, Parmesan cheese, ricotta cheese, and pepper together until smooth. Add the sautéed ham and scallions to the cheese mixture; then add the eggs and mix well. Cover and refrigerate at least 2 or 3 hours.

Spread half the filling on one pasta sheet, leaving a half-inch border. Brush the ends with melted butter. Arrange a layer of sliced prosciutto over the filling to cover. Beginning at one of the short ends of the pasta, roll it up. (Do not roll too loosely or the poaching liquid may seep into the cheese/meat mixture.) Wrap the roll in a double thickness of cheesecloth and tie each end securely with string. Repeat for the second pasta sheet. Fill a large, deep sauté pan with chicken stock. Bring to a boil and add the pasta rolls. Reduce the heat to a simmer and cook gently, turning the rolls occasionally, for 25 minutes. Drain and cool before removing string and cheesecloth.

Cut each roll in half-inch-thick slices and arrange on plates. Pour tomato sauce on each plate and add chives. Serve warm or at room temperature.

NOTE: If being served at room temperature, the rolls can be poached up to 2 days in advance and refrigerated in the cheesecloth. Slice them chilled and allow them to reach room temperature before serving.

SERVES 6 TO 8

WILD MUSHROOM RISOTTO

LIDIA BASTIANICH, NEW YORK, NEW YORK

There is really no mystery to perfect risotto; it results from lovingly stirring the rice as it absorbs the liquid and gains a creamy consistency from the starch that is released into the stock. This dish is flavored with earthy wild mushrooms, and the flavor is amplified by the dried porcini.

1 tablespoon dried porcini mushrooms
5 tablespoons olive oil
Salt and freshly ground black pepper
1 cup minced onion
2 tablespoons minced shallots
³/₄ pound mixed wild mushrooms (such as shiitake, chanterelles, porcini, oyster mushrooms), cleaned and sliced
2 cups arborio rice
¹/₂ cup dry white wine
6¹/₂ cups hot chicken stock, preferably homemade (pages 26–28)
2 tablespoons unsalted butter, cut into bits
¹/₂ cup freshly grated Parmesan cheese

JEREMIAH TOWER
CHEF AND OWNER, STARS CAFE,
SAN FRANCISCO, CA

Why did you become a chef?
I became a chef because I was broke and someone offered me a job.

How did you receive your training?
My training was as a customer on luxury ships and in the best hotels and restaurants in the world.

Any tips to pass on?
Hire someone to clean up the kitchen.

Soak the dried mushrooms in ½ cup hot water for 20 minutes. Drain and chop the mushrooms, reserving the mushroom water as well as the mushrooms.

In a medium sauté pan or skillet, heat 2 tablespoons of the olive oil over medium-high heat. Add the rehydrated mushrooms and sauté them for 4 to 5 minutes, stirring frequently, or until they are brown and soft. Sprinkle with salt and pepper and set aside.

Heat the remaining 3 tablespoons of olive oil in a medium saucepan over medium heat. Add the onion and shallots and sauté, stirring frequently, for 3 to 4 minutes, or until golden. Stir in the mixed wild mushrooms and sauté until they are golden. Add the rice to the pan, and stir to coat. Cook for 2 minutes, stirring constantly, until the rice is opaque.

Add the wine, ½ cup of hot broth, and ½ teaspoon salt. Cook, stirring constantly, until all the liquid is absorbed. Add the sautéed mushrooms, rehydrated mushrooms, and reserved mushroom water, and stir until the liquid is almost absorbed. Continue to add the hot stock by ½-cup amounts, and cook until each successive addition has been absorbed before adding the next, stirring almost constantly. This will take approximately 20 minutes.

When all the stock has been added, the rice should be al dente and the dish should be creamy. Remove the risotto from the heat. Stir in the butter and cheese and season with salt and pepper. Serve the risotto hot.

NOTE: Arborio rice is a species of short, fat grains that give off the starch necessary to create a creamy risotto. It can be found in specialty food stores and most supermarkets.

SERVES 4 AS AN ENTRÉE, 6 AS AN APPETIZER

SMOKED TOMATO AND SHIITAKE MUSHROOM RISOTTO

MICHAEL UDDO, NEW ORLEANS, LOUISIANA

The smoked nuance of the tomatoes adds an exciting flavor to this risotto dish. Do a few batches of tomatoes at a time, and freeze the remainder for future renditions of this stunning appetizer.

1 cup wood chips (mesquite, apple, pecan, or some combination)
2 medium ripe tomatoes
$1/4$ cup olive oil
1 cup minced onion
2 tablespoons minced shallots
2 cups arborio rice
$1/2$ cup dry white wine
$6^{1}/_{2}$ cups hot chicken stock, preferably homemade (pages 26–28)
$1^{1}/_{2}$ teaspoons salt
$1/3$ cup ($2/3$ stick) unsalted butter
8 shiitake mushrooms, thinly sliced
3 tablespoons minced fresh chives
3 tablespoons minced fresh parsley
Salt and freshly ground black pepper

Light a charcoal fire and soak the wood chips in water to cover. Brush the tomatoes with 1 tablespoon of the olive oil. Push the coals to one side of the grill. Place the drained wood chips on medium-hot coals and place the tomatoes as far away from the coals as possible. Smoke with the top closed for 15 to 20 minutes, or until tomatoes are soft and slightly charred. Remove the tomatoes from the grill, and when cool enough to handle, remove the skin, chop the tomatoes, and drain.

In a medium flameproof casserole, heat the remaining 3 tablespoons olive oil and sauté the onion and shallots until golden, about 4 to 5 minutes. Add the rice to the shallots, and stir to coat with oil. Cook the rice to toast to a light golden color, stirring constantly, about 5 to 6 minutes.

Add the wine, stir well, and then add $1/2$ cup of the hot chicken stock and the salt. Cook, stirring constantly, until all the liquid is absorbed. Continue to add hot stock in small batches (just enough to moisten rice completely) and cook until each successive batch of the hot stock has been absorbed and the risotto is creamy but still al dente.

In a medium sauté pan over medium heat, melt the butter. Add the tomatoes and mushrooms, and cook for 2 minutes. Add the tomatoes and mushrooms to the cooked rice. Cook, stirring constantly, for 3 minutes. Add the chives and parsley and season with salt and pepper. Serve immediately.

NOTE: The tomatoes can be smoked up to 2 days in advance and refrigerated, tightly covered. The risotto must be made just prior to serving.

SERVES 4

CHEF'S TIP

Leftover risotto can be turned into fritters by frying walnut-size pieces in hot vegetable oil. For a variation, press the cold rice around cubes of mozzarella cheese.

RISOTTO WITH PROSCIUTTO AND VEGETABLES

FERNANDO SARACCHI, NEW ORLEANS, LOUISIANA

1 bunch (10 ounces) spinach
1/4 pound (1 stick) unsalted butter
1/2 cup chopped onion
2 cups arborio rice
1 cup white wine
6 cups simmering chicken stock, preferably homemade (pages 26–28)
2/3 cup finely chopped carrots
2/3 cup finely chopped prosciutto, plus 12 slices
1/2 cup diced fresh porcini mushrooms
1/3 cup fresh peas
1 cup freshly grated Parmesan cheese
Salt and freshly ground black pepper

Rinse and stem the spinach. Blanch the spinach in boiling water for 2 minutes, then drain well and purée in a blender or food processor. Set aside.

Heat the butter in a saucepan over medium heat. Add the onion and sauté for 3 minutes, or until it is translucent. Add the rice and cook for 3 minutes. Raise the heat to high, add the wine, and cook, stirring constantly, until it has almost evaporated. Add 1/2 cup of the stock, and stir over medium heat constantly until the stock has been absorbed by the rice. Continue adding stock 1/2 cup at a time, and after 2 cups have been absorbed, add the carrots, chopped prosciutto, mushrooms, and spinach purée. When all but 1 cup of the stock has been added, add the peas and continue to cook until all the stock has been incorporated and the dish has a creamy consistency.

Stir in the cheese, add salt and pepper to taste, and serve immediately with 2 slices of prosciutto on the sides of each bowl.

NOTE: The spinach purée can be made up to 1 day in advance and refrigerated, tightly covered. The remainder of the dish must be cooked just prior to serving.

SERVES 6

FISH AND SEAFOOD

ENTREÉS WITH AN ITALIAN ACCENT

Italy and the United States share the geographic serendipity
of being surrounded by waters that support a rich variety
of fish and shellfish, which are playing an increasingly
important role in the diets of both nations.
The key to cooking all fish is "less is more." Fish should be
cooked so that it remains slightly translucent in the center,
since it continues to cook after being removed from the
heat source. Fish such as tuna and swordfish toughen
terribly if overcooked, and should be kept slightly rare.
A good rule of thumb is that fish steaks and fillets should
cook 10 minutes for each inch of thickness, so the total time
for cooking a fillet is probably just 4 to 5 minutes.
The same is true for crustaceans such as shrimp
and lobster; overcooking diminishes their sweet
flavor and tender texture.
While Italians also grill fish, their most frequent
cooking method is a simple sauté, and that is
reflected in the recipes in this chapter.

GROUPER WITH TOMATO SAUCE

Tom Weaver, New Orleans, Louisiana

Grouper is a sea bass with mild, white, lean flesh. In this recipe, it is simply prepared in a zesty tomato sauce.

SAUCE

2 tablespoons olive oil
4 small onions, peeled and cut into large dice
2 small bell peppers, cut into large dice
3 stalks celery, cut into medium dice
1 1/2 teaspoons minced garlic
2 large fresh tomatoes, peeled, seeded, and diced (page 30)
1 teaspoon minced fresh thyme
1 teaspoon minced fresh oregano
1 teaspoon minced fresh basil
1/2 cup dry white wine
3/4 cup fish stock or bottled clam juice
1 1/4 cups tomato purée
1/8 teaspoon dried red pepper flakes
Pinch cayenne pepper
Salt and freshly ground black pepper

FISH

3 pounds fresh grouper fillets, cut into 8-ounce portions
1 pound medium shrimp, peeled and deveined

To make the sauce, heat the olive oil in a medium saucepan. Add the onions, bell peppers, and celery, and cook over medium heat until tender, about 5 minutes. Add the garlic, tomatoes, thyme, oregano, basil, white wine, and fish stock or clam juice, and simmer for about 10 minutes. Add the tomato purée, red pepper flakes, cayenne pepper, salt, and black pepper and simmer for about 30 minutes, or until thick. Set aside.

Preheat the oven to 400°F. Place about 3 cups of the sauce in the bottom of a large ovenproof sauté pan or skillet or heatproof casserole. Place the fish fillets over the sauce, and put equal amounts of shrimp on top of each fish fillet. Top the shrimp with the remaining sauce. Heat over high heat until the sauce simmers. Cover and bake for about 12 minutes, or until the fillets begin to flake. Arrange the fillets and shrimp on 6 warm plates.

NOTE: The sauce can be made up to 3 days in advance and refrigerated, tightly covered. Reheat it gently over low heat before baking the fish.

SERVES 6

TUNA WITH OLIVE SAUCE

EMERIL LAGASSE, NEW ORLEANS, LOUISIANA

This is a lusty treatment for a fish as hearty and meaty as tuna—called the "vegetarian's filet mignon." It can also be served at room temperature or chilled as part of a buffet.

4 yellowfin tuna fillets, 5 to 6 ounces each
¹/₂ teaspoon dried oregano
¹/₂ teaspoon dried thyme
Pinch of cayenne pepper
Salt and freshly ground black pepper
All-purpose flour for dredging
1 tablespoon olive oil
¹/₂ red bell pepper, seeds and ribs removed, and finely diced
    (pages 8–9)
¹/₂ green bell pepper, seeds and ribs removed, and finely diced
    (pages 8–9)
1 medium onion, peeled and diced
1 stalk celery, diced
Pinch of crushed dried red pepper
3 garlic cloves, peeled and minced
¹/₂ cup pitted and halved black olives
¹/₂ cup pitted and halved green olives
2 teaspoons chopped fresh parsley
4 anchovy fillets, finely chopped
2 tomatoes, peeled, seeded, and chopped (page 30)
6 tablespoons (³/₄ stick) unsalted butter
¹/₄ cup olive oil

Rinse the fish and pat dry. Combine the oregano, thyme, and cayenne with salt and pepper. Sprinkle on the fish, and then dredge the fillets in flour, shaking off any excess.

Heat the 1 tablespoon olive oil in a large sauté pan over high heat. Sear the tuna fillets to medium-rare, about 2 minutes per side. Remove from the pan and reserve in a warm place. Degrease the pan and return it to the heat. When it is hot, add the red and green bell peppers, onion, and celery. Season with crushed dried red pepper. Sauté until the vegetables begin to turn translucent. Add the garlic, black and green olives, and chopped parsley. Cook for a few seconds, then stir in the anchovies and tomatoes.

To finish the sauce, beat in the butter, a couple of tablespoons at a time, then add ¼ cup olive oil. Taste and adjust the seasoning with salt and pepper.

Return the tuna to the pan to rewarm, spooning the sauce and vegetables on top of the fillets. Serve the tuna topped with sauce.

NOTE: The tuna can be seared and the sauce can be completed 1 day in advance and refrigerated, tightly covered. Reheat the sauce over low heat, and then reheat the tuna in the sauce.

SERVES 4

CHEF'S TIP

When searing any fish steak or fillet, chill it in the freezer for 10 minutes before cooking and the center will remain rare.

GARLIC-CRUSTED TROUT WITH SWEET PEPPER AND SHRIMP SAUCE

JAY KIMBALL, NEW ORLEANS, LOUISIANA

The crisp garlic bread crumb crust preserves the moistness of tender trout fillets without deep-frying, and the tart sauce is a perfect foil to the fish. This method can be used for many dishes that are more often fried.

SAUCE

1 tablespoon extra-virgin olive oil
1 tomato, peeled and finely diced (page 30)
1 roasted red pepper, peeled, seeded, deribbed, and finely diced
   (pages 8–9)
¹/₃ cup finely diced onion
1 teaspoon salt
Pinch cayenne pepper
1 teaspoon fresh lemon juice
1 teaspoon fresh lime juice
¹/₄ cup shrimp stock or bottled clam juice
12 to 15 large shrimp
¹/₃ cup shredded fresh basil

COATING

2 tablespoons grated Romano cheese
1 teaspoon salt
1 teaspoon black pepper
1 teaspoon minced garlic
1 teaspoon minced fresh thyme
1 teaspoon minced fresh parsley
¹/₃ loaf stale French bread, cubed (2 cups)

FISH

4 skinless trout fillets
3 tablespoons extra-virgin olive oil

To make the sauce, in a large sauté pan or skillet over medium heat, heat the olive oil and sauté the tomato, red pepper, onion, salt, and cayenne for 1 minute. Add the lemon and lime juices and the shrimp stock. Cook over medium heat until reduced by half, about 4 minutes. Cut the shrimp in half lengthwise. Add the shrimp and basil to the sauce. Cook until the shrimp turn pink, about 2 to 3 minutes. Set aside and keep warm.

To coat and cook the fish, preheat the oven to 500°F. Place all the ingredients for the coating in a blender or food processor and blend until fine. Spread the coating on wax paper and press the trout fillets firmly into it to coat evenly. In a large ovenproof sauté pan or skillet, heat the 3 tablespoons olive oil to smoking and cook the fillets on each side until browned, about 2 minutes per side. Put in the oven and bake for 4 to 5 minutes, or until the crust is crisp.

To serve, place 1 fillet on each of 4 serving plates and surround with the sweet pepper and shrimp sauce.

NOTE: The sauce and coating can be prepared up to 1 day in advance and refrigerated, tightly covered. The fish should be cooked just prior to serving.

SERVES 4

POACHED FISH
WITH TOMATOES AND
PURPLE BASIL

JEREMIAH TOWER, SAN FRANCISCO, CALIFORNIA

While purple basil has a distinctive flavor as well as color, there is no reason why this easy and aromatic dish cannot be done with green basil. Any firm-fleshed fish fillet such as grouper, snapper, or flounder can be used in place of the halibut; adjust the cooking time if the fillet is thinner than ¹/₂ inch.

4 halibut fillets, 6 ounces each
¹/₂ pound (2 sticks) unsalted butter
2 cups fish stock (pages 26–29)
Salt and freshly ground black pepper
2 cups skinned, seeded, and chopped tomatoes (page 30)
2 cups chopped purple basil

Remove the skin from the fish fillets. In a large sauté pan, melt 4 tablespoons (¹/₂ stick) of the butter, add the fish, and cover with fish stock. Season with salt and pepper. Cover the fish with buttered parchment paper, then bring to a boil and simmer for about 2 minutes. Turn the fish and cook an additional 2 minutes. Remove from the heat, remove the paper, and let rest for about 1 minute.

Remove the fish from the pan with a slotted spatula and drain on paper towels. Pass the fish stock through a strainer into another sauté pan; bring to a boil over high heat and reduce by one-third. Add the tomatoes and basil to the pan, heat through, then add the remaining 1¹/₂ sticks butter, salt, and pepper, and whisk. Place the fish on serving plates, spoon the sauce over, and garnish with basil leaves.

NOTE: This dish can be done up to 2 hours in advance and kept at room temperature. Reheat the fish gently in the sauce just prior to serving.

SERVES 4

RED SNAPPER WITH ARTICHOKE AND MUSHROOMS

JOAQUIN GONZALEZ, SAN ANTONIO, TEXAS

Simple pan-fried fish with artichoke hearts and mushrooms can be served with an interesting pasta or risotto and a green salad for a quick and lovely dinner.

4 red snapper fillets, 6 ounces each
1 cup vegetable oil
1 egg
1 cup milk
Salt and freshly ground black pepper
All-purpose flour for dredging
6 to 8 tablespoons (³/₄ to 1 stick) unsalted butter
4 to 5 mushrooms, washed and sliced
3 artichoke hearts, cooked and sliced
Juice of 1 lemon

Wash the fillets and pat dry. Heat the vegetable oil in a sauté pan or skillet over medium-high heat. In a bowl, beat the egg, milk, and salt and pepper to taste and dip the fillets in the mixture. Dredge in flour and fry in the hot oil, turning after 2 minutes, for a total cooking time of 4 to 5 minutes. Remove the fillets with a slotted spatula and drain on paper towels.

Pour the grease out of the pan and add the butter. Add the mushrooms and artichoke hearts and sauté for 5 minutes, stirring gently. Add the lemon juice, sprinkle with salt and pepper, and divide the vegetables and sauce on top of the fillets.

NOTE: The dish can be prepared up to 1 hour in advance. Reheat the fish in the sauce.

SERVES 4

PAN-ROASTED SNAPPER WITH ROASTED GARLIC AND SUN-DRIED TOMATO BUTTER

FRANK BRIGTSEN, NEW ORLEANS, LOUISIANA

The nutty taste of roasted garlic pairs very well with tangy sun-dried tomatoes. In addition to this fish dish, the butter would also be great topping anything from grilled chicken to bread.

BUTTER

1 cup (2 sticks) unsalted butter, at room temperature
¼ cup finely chopped oil-packed sun-dried tomatoes
¼ teaspoon salt
1 teaspoon minced fresh basil
⅛ teaspoon cayenne pepper
2 tablespoons roasted garlic (pages 13–14)

FISH

6 snapper fillets with skin, 7 ounces each
Salt and freshly ground black pepper
1 cup all-purpose flour
½ cup clarified butter (page 11)
1 cup fish stock or bottled clam juice

To make the butter, blend all the ingredients until smooth in a blender or food processor. Refrigerate until ready to serve.

To prepare the fish, preheat the oven to 450°F. Season each snapper fillet lightly with salt and pepper and dust the skin side of each fillet with flour. Heat 2 large ovenproof sauté pans or skillets over medium-high heat and add ¼ cup clarified butter to each. Place the fish in the hot butter, skin side down, and cook for 1 minute. Put in the oven and bake for 7 to 8 minutes, or until the fish begins to flake.

Place a fillet on each of 6 heated plates. Discard the clarified butter and return the sauté pans or skillets to high heat. Add ½ cup of stock or clam juice to each pan and bring to a boil. Add half of the garlic and tomato butter to each pan and cook until the butter is almost melted, about 1 to 2 minutes. Serve the sauce on top of the fish.

NOTE: The butter may be prepared up to 3 days in advance and refrigerated, tightly covered; it can also be frozen for up to 3 months.

SERVES 6

CHEF'S TIP

Roasted garlic can be frozen for up to 3 months, and is a wonderful addition to anything from simple mashed potatoes to the meat from which hamburgers are made.

DOVER SOLE MEDUSA

KEVIN GRAHAM, NEW ORLEANS, LOUISIANA

While this is a show-stopping presentation, with curled coils of fish still attached at the tail, the dish will be just as delicious with less fanfare and work if the fillets are merely poached. The capers and fried fennel are a wonderful flavor accent to the delicate fish.

4 Dover sole (or flounder), about 1 pound each, cleaned and scaled
4 cups fish stock (pages 26–29) or bottled clam juice
$^1/_2$ cup olive oil
4 fresh fennel sprigs
Salt and freshly ground black pepper
$1^1/_2$ cups beurre blanc sauce (pages 9–10)
$^1/_4$ cup nonpareil capers, drained and rinsed

Skin the sole and remove the heads. Using the point of a sharp knife, cut through the flesh along the side fins. Working at an angle, with the knife almost flat, cut the flesh away from the ribs. Turn the fish over and repeat the process to end up with 2 whole fillets still attached to the fish at the tail. Beginning 2 inches from the tail, cut both fillets into 8 lengthwise strips. Repeat with the remaining sole.

In a large saucepan, bring the fish stock or clam juice to a rolling boil. Holding 1 sole by the tail, carefully lower the fish into the simmering stock. The strips should curl gently. Cook for 1 to 2 minutes, then remove the fish from the pan and drain on paper towels. Repeat with the remaining fish. Keep warm. In a small, heavy saucepan, heat the olive oil to 350°F. and cook the fennel sprigs just until crisp, about 2 to 3 minutes. Remove from the pan and drain on paper towels.

Season the fish with salt and pepper and arrange a pair of fillets on each of 4 plates with the tail at 12 o'clock. Surround the fish with beurre blanc sauce. Sprinkle the capers over the sole and garnish with the deep-fried fennel sprigs.

NOTE: The fish can be prepared up to poaching a few hours in advance and refrigerated, tightly covered with plastic wrap.

SERVES 4

GRILLED CHILEAN SEA BASS WITH DILL GREMOLATA

DOUGLAS DALE, LAKE TAHOE, NEVADA

Gremolata is the mixture of fresh herbs and lemon zest traditionally used on Italian ossobuco. Here we have a cross-cultural dish, with Scandinavian dill in the mixture, and Asian tamari in the sauce.

4 pounds Chilean sea bass fillets, cut into 8-ounce sections (striped bass, grouper, black cod, bluefish, or any other oily fish fillets may be substituted)

GREMOLATA
5 tablespoons chopped fresh dill
1 tablespoon grated lemon zest
2 garlic cloves, blanched in boiling water for 5 minutes, then peeled and crushed
5 tablespoons freshly grated Parmesan cheese
5 sun-dried tomato halves, boiled for 10 minutes to soften, then minced

BASTING SAUCE
¹/₂ cup soybean oil
¹/₃ cup olive oil
¹/₃ cup tamari

Rinse the fish in cold water, pat with paper towels, and set aside. Mix all of the gremolata ingredients together in a small bowl and set aside. Mix the basting sauce and set aside.

Light a charcoal grill or preheat a broiler. Place the fish on a rack. Baste with the basting liquid and grill for 4 to 5 minutes on a side over hot coals or under a hot broiler, depending on the thickness of the fillets. Top with the gremolata and serve at once.

NOTE: All the parts of the recipe except the fish can be prepared earlier on the day of service and reheated as appropriate. The fish should be grilled at the last minute.

SERVES 8

FISH STEW WITH FENNEL

GUNTER PREUSS, NEW ORLEANS, LOUISIANA

Fresh fennel, tasting of licorice, is a favorite Italian accompaniment to fish and seafood dishes. This hearty soup is a meal in itself. Serve it with bread and a salad.

STOCK

4 medium carrots, peeled and sliced
2 onions, peeled and sliced
6 celery stalks, sliced
2 leeks (white part only), sliced
2 medium green peppers, seeds and ribs removed, and sliced (pages 8–9)
2 fennel roots, cleaned, stripped of darkened leaves, and chopped
$1/4$ cup ($1/2$ stick) unsalted butter
2 tablespoons tomato paste
1 cup brandy
2 cups white wine
3 tomatoes, peeled, seeded, and chopped (page 30)
1 teaspoon minced garlic
$1/2$ teaspoon saffron threads, crushed
3 quarts fish stock (pages 26–29)

FISH AND SHELLFISH

1 teaspoon chopped shallots
1 teaspoon chopped garlic
1 teaspoon chopped green onion
1 teaspoon minced parsley
2 tablespoons olive oil
1 pound shrimp, peeled and deveined
1 pound boneless, skinless fish fillets, cut into 1-inch pieces
6 oysters, shucked (pages 17–18)
6 medium lobster tails, shelled
$1/2$ cup brandy, heated gently
2 cups white wine
Salt and freshly ground black pepper
$1/4$ pound lump crabmeat
Salt and freshly ground black pepper

In a large, deep skillet or sauté pan sauté the carrots, onions, celery, leeks, peppers, and fennel in the butter until translucent. Add the tomato paste. Sauté briefly, then flame with brandy. Extinguish the flames with the white wine. Add the tomatoes, garlic, and saffron. Add the fish broth. Simmer until the vegetables are tender, approximately 30 minutes.

Sauté the shallots, garlic, green onion, and parsley in the olive oil in a stockpot for 1 minute. Add the shrimp, fish fillet pieces, oysters, and lobster and sear for about 1 minute. Flame with the heated brandy. Add the white wine. Add the prepared fish stock and simmer for approximately 5 minutes. Add salt and pepper to taste. Top with fresh lump crabmeat.

NOTE: The stock can be prepared up to 3 days in advance and refrigerated. The fish should be cooked and added just prior to serving.

SERVES 6

GOFFREDO FRACCARO
CHEF AND OWNER, LA RIVIERA, METAIRIE, LA

Why did you become a chef?
I wanted to be a maestro!

How did you receive your training?
I was still in my teens when I was an apprentice at the Columbia Hotel in Genoa and then worked as chef for the Italian Line of luxury ocean liners.

Any tips to pass on?
I plant fresh herbs in my garden at home, and before winter I gather them and freeze them. This is much better than using dried herbs for cooking.

SCAMPI

GOFFREDO FRACCARO, NEW ORLEANS, LOUISIANA

Scampi, actually the Italian word for a specific large prawn, was one of the first Italian dishes to become popular in this country. It is a quick sauté, and needs some bread to soak up the sauce and a salad to make it a meal.

2 pounds large raw shrimp, peeled and deveined, with tails left on
Salt and freshly ground black pepper
3 tablespoons olive oil
1 tablespoon paprika
1 garlic clove, peeled and chopped
1 teaspoon chopped fresh oregano
1 teaspoon chopped parsley, plus additional for garnish
1 teaspoon chopped basil
1 teaspoon chopped mint
1 lemon, juiced, plus lemon wedges for garnish
¼ cup water
½ cup (1 stick) unsalted butter

Place a large sauté pan over high heat. Place the shrimp in a sauté pan with salt, pepper, and olive oil. Toss, sprinkle with paprika, and cook, covered, on top of the stove for about 2 minutes.

Drain off the oil and add the garlic, oregano, 1 teaspoon chopped parsley, basil, mint, lemon juice, and water. Swirl in the butter. Cook over medium-high heat for 3 minutes, or until the shrimp are pink. Correct the seasonings and serve garnished with chopped parsley and lemon wedges.

NOTE: The dish should be cooked just prior to serving; however the ingredients can be organized a few hours in advance and kept at room temperature.

SERVES 4

GRILLED PESTO SHRIMP

Randy Windham, New Orleans, Louisiana

Aromatic pesto, heady with garlic and fresh basil, is used here both as a sauce and as a marinade. The shrimp absorb its flavor, and they serve as a textural foil to the creamy polenta.

20 large shrimp, peeled and deveined
Basic Pesto Sauce (page 175)
Creamy Polenta (page 169)
1 tablespoon balsamic vinegar
1 tablespoon basil-flavored olive oil (available at specialty food stores, or see Chef's Tip)
4 teaspoons freshly grated Parmesan cheese
1 tablespoon minced fresh chives

Put the shrimp in a medium mixing bowl. Toss with the pesto sauce and marinate at room temperature for 30 minutes.

Light a charcoal or gas grill and when the coals are covered with gray ash, grill the shrimp for about 2 to 3 minutes on each side. Divide the polenta among 4 large flat-rimmed soup dishes. Place the shrimp on top and sprinkle with balsamic vinegar and basil-flavored oil. Sprinkle with Parmesan cheese and chives.

NOTE: Strips of boneless skinless chicken breast or fish fillets can be treated in the same fashion.

SERVES 4

CHEF'S TIP

While basil oil is commercially available, it is easy to make any herb oil at home. To infuse an oil, finely chop the flavoring ingredient and combine with the olive oil. (For herbs, add ³/₄ cup chopped herb to 1 pint of olive oil.) Allow the mixture to stand for a minimum of 48 hours refrigerated. If you use the oil for sautéing, the flavor particles should be strained out, but they can be left in for dressings.

SHRIMP WITH PERNOD

MOLLY McCALL, TUCSON, ARIZONA

This quickly sautéed shrimp dish, creamy yet tasting of heady anise-flavored Pernod, can become a pasta sauce; then all the meal needs is a green salad.

18 large shrimp
3 tablespoons olive oil
3 tablespoons green peppercorns, packed in brine, drained and
    rinsed
¹/₂ cup chopped green onions, white part only
1 large shallot, peeled and chopped
¹/₂ cup Pernod
1 cup heavy cream
¹/₂ cup sour cream
Salt and freshly ground black pepper

Peel and devein the shrimp, leaving the tails on. Butterfly them by cutting down the curved ridge but not all the way through the shrimp. Flatten them slightly between 2 sheets of wax paper, and set aside.

Heat the olive oil in a sauté pan or skillet over medium-high heat. Add the shrimp and sauté 1 minute. Stir in the peppercorns and add the green onions and shallot, sautéing 1 minute more. Add the Pernod and reduce by half over high heat.

Remove the shrimp from the pan with a slotted spoon. Stir the heavy cream and sour cream into the sauce and reduce over medium-high heat until thick enough to coat the back of a spoon, about 7 minutes. Return the shrimp to the pan, season with salt and pepper to taste, and serve immediately.

NOTE: The dish can be prepared up to a few hours in advance and reheated gently over low heat.

SERVES 3

SAUTÉED SOFT-SHELL CRABS

CHARLES PALMER, NEW YORK, NEW YORK

This easy-to-prepare dish is a stunning way to enjoy the delicacy of soft-shell crabs. Serve this with some sautéed zucchini or summer squash so that the vegetable is not too assertive, and polenta cakes.

8 soft-shell crabs, cleaned (pages 11–12)
Salt and freshly ground black pepper
All-purpose flour for dredging the crabs
1/2 cup vegetable oil
3 tablespoons unsalted butter
Juice of 1 lemon
1 teaspoon minced fresh parsley
1/2 teaspoon minced fresh chives
1/2 teaspoon minced fresh tarragon
Polenta Cakes (page 170)

Pat the crabs dry and season with salt and pepper. Coat the crabs with the flour and set aside.

In a large sauté pan or skillet heat the vegetable oil over medium heat. Add the crabs, top shells down, and fry for 2 minutes. Turn the crabs and cook for another 2 minutes. Remove the crabs and drain on paper towels.

Add the butter to the pan that held the crabs, increase the heat to high, and cook until the butter is browned but not burned. Add the lemon juice, parsley, chives, and tarragon. Check the sauce for seasoning and adjust with salt and pepper if necessary.

To assemble, arrange 2 polenta cakes on each plate and top with 2 crabs each. Spoon the lemon herb butter over each portion and serve.

NOTE: This dish can be done with large shrimp or fish fillets in place of the soft-shell crabs.

SERVES 4

WOOD-GRILLED LOBSTER WITH TOASTED WALNUTS

TODD ENGLISH, CHARLESTOWN, MASSACHUSETTS

This is a stunning lobster dish: The flavor from the grilling and slight smoking becomes an undertone, one reinforced by the toasted nuts. The chef serves this with potato gnocchi, small potato dumplings. If you don't want to make them, they can be purchased frozen in many markets, or the dish is just as delicious if served with fresh pasta.

1 cup applewood chips
4 live lobsters, 1½ pounds each
Salt and freshly ground black pepper
2 tablespoons olive oil
1 cup (2 sticks) unsalted butter
2 cups finely chopped walnuts
Julienned zest of 1 lemon
½ bunch fresh parsley, stemmed and minced
Freshly grated Parmesan cheese
Potato Gnocchi (page 172)

To prepare the lobster, light a charcoal grill; meanwhile, soak the applewood chips in cold water to cover. Kill the lobsters by inserting a knife at the base of the body, and cut off the tails and claws; reserve the bodies and knuckles for making stock.

Cut the lobster tails in half lengthwise with a heavy sharp knife, and set aside. Bring a medium stockpot of lightly salted water to a boil and boil the claws for 3 minutes. Drain the claws and place them in a bowl of ice water to stop further cooking.

Coat the shells of the lobster tails and the lobster claws with the olive oil. When the fire is hot (the coals are still bright red), drain the soaked wood chips and place them on top of the coals. Grill the split lobster meat over a hot wood-charcoal fire for 4 to 5 minutes. Remove the cooked lobster from the grill.

Melt the butter in a medium saucepan and add the walnuts. Cook over medium heat until the walnuts are toasted, about 3 to 4 minutes.

Pull the lobster meat from the tail section and add, along with the boiled claw meat still in the shell, to the butter-walnut mixture, tossing to coat well.

Sprinkle the lobster meat and claws with the lemon zest, pepper, and minced parsley. Sprinkle the finished dish with Parmesan cheese and add the drained gnocchi. To serve, arrange the lobster on plates with the gnocchi.

NOTE: The lobster can be grilled up to 4 hours in advance.

SERVES 4

CHEF'S TIP

For those weak of heart about killing lobsters, the entire lobster can be plunged into boiling water for 1 minute, at which time it will be dead. Remove the lobster with tongs, cut off the tail, and return the claws to the pot to continue cooking.

POULTRY AND GAME BIRD ENTRÉES:

SIMPLE AND SPLENDID

If the professional kitchen can be compared to a painter's studio, then poultry would be the best blank canvas on which to work. From subtle chicken that takes well to all seasonings to rich duck or toothsome game birds, poultry is a favorite in every cuisine.

It is only in the past few years that American home cooks have had access to feathered game such as pheasant and squab, and using them is not yet spontaneous, since except in a few major cities, they must be ordered for overnight delivery.

In Northern Italian cooking, game birds are used more frequently than simple chicken and they should be served with the hearty red wines of the region, such as Barolo or Barbaresco.

SCALOPPINE OF CHICKEN WITH STIR-FRIED VEGETABLES

ANDRÉ POIROT, NEW ORLEANS, LOUISIANA

This fast and easy dish is low in fat but not in flavor or visual appeal. Cutting the pesto sauce with yogurt creates a delicious, creamy sauce.

6 small new red potatoes, halved
4 skinless, boneless chicken breast halves
6 tablespoons flour, for dredging
1 teaspoon salt
1 teaspoon pepper
¼ cup olive oil
2 cups mixed julienned carrots, zucchini, and yellow squash
2 tablespoons dry white wine
4 tablespoons Basic Pesto Sauce (page 175)
2 tablespoons plain low-fat yogurt
2 teaspoons minced fresh chives

Cook the potatoes in boiling salted water to cover until tender, about 7 to 8 minutes; drain and set aside. Meanwhile, with the flat side of a meat mallet or the bottom of a heavy bottle, pound the chicken breasts until flattened. Mix together the flour, salt, and pepper. Lightly dredge the chicken in the seasoned flour. In a medium sauté pan or skillet, heat 2 tablespoons of the olive oil and sauté the chicken for 2 to 3 minutes on each side, or until opaque throughout. Set aside and keep warm.

In another medium sauté pan or skillet, heat the remaining 2 tablespoons olive oil and sauté the vegetables until crisp-tender, about 3 to 4 minutes. Mix the wine, pesto, yogurt, and chives in a small saucepan and heat through. Serve each breast with some of the potatoes and vegetables, and drizzle the pesto mixture over the chicken.

NOTE: The potatoes can be boiled and the vegetables can be cut up to a few hours in advance and kept at room temperature. However, the dish should be cooked just prior to serving.

SERVES 4

CHICKEN WITH PINK AND GREEN PEPPERCORNS

René Verdon, San Francisco, California

This is an easy and elegant dish for a party. The flavorful stuffing, dotted with crushed pink and green peppercorns, is under the crisp skin of the chicken breasts.

Chicken
4 boneless chicken breast halves, skin on
¹/₄ cup Cognac
1 teaspoon fresh thyme
1 small bay leaf, crushed
Salt and freshly ground black pepper

Stuffing
1 slice white bread, crusts removed
¹/₂ cup heavy cream
¹/₂ teaspoon dried green peppercorns
¹/₂ teaspoon dried pink peppercorns
¹/₂ cup ground veal
4 large shiitake mushrooms, stemmed and finely diced
Pinch of ground nutmeg
Salt and freshly ground white pepper

Marinate the chicken breasts for 1 hour in the mixture of Cognac, thyme, bay leaf, salt, and pepper.

To make the stuffing, soak the bread in heavy cream and crush the peppercorns in a mortar and pestle. In a bowl, mix the ground veal and mushrooms with the bread and cream mixture, peppercorns, nutmeg, salt, and pepper.

Preheat the oven to 375°F. Drain the chicken breasts and pat dry. Place 2 heaping tablespoons of stuffing under the skin of each breast. Bake for 35 to 40 minutes. Serve immediately.

NOTE: The stuffing can be prepared up to 1 day in advance and refrigerated, tightly covered. Do not stuff the breasts until just prior to serving.

SERVES 4

CHICKEN WITH ARTICHOKES AND MUSHROOMS

JOAQUIN GONZALEZ, SAN ANTONIO, TEXAS

1 frying chicken (3 pounds)
1 cup vegetable oil
1 egg
1 cup milk
Salt and freshly ground black pepper
All-purpose flour for dredging
4 large mushrooms, washed, stemmed, and sliced
1/2 cup (1 stick) unsalted butter
4 artichoke hearts, cooked and sliced
1/4 cup dry white wine
1 tablespoon chopped green onions, white part only

Bone the chicken and remove the skin, reserving the skin and bones for making stock. Cut the meat into 3-inch chunks and pound them slightly so they are all of uniform thickness.

Heat the vegetable oil in a sauté pan or skillet over medium-high heat. Beat the egg with the milk and a sprinkling of salt and pepper, and dip the chicken pieces in the mixture. Then dredge in flour, shaking to remove the excess, and place the chicken in the pan, being careful not to crowd the pieces.

Brown the chicken on one side, about 4 minutes, then turn with tongs and add the mushrooms to the pan. Cook for 2 minutes, then place the mushrooms on top of the chicken pieces so they will not overcook. Cook 2 minutes longer.

Pour the grease out of the pan and add the butter and artichoke hearts. Sauté gently for 2 minutes, then add the white wine and green onions and reduce slightly for 2 minutes. Turn off the heat, cover the pan, and allow the mixture to steam for 5 minutes. Adjust the seasoning.

NOTE: While the chef used a whole chicken in this recipe, skinning and boning it himself, boned and skinned chicken breasts, 2 halves per person, could easily be substituted.

SERVES 4

CAPON WITH ROSEMARY

JACK MCDAVID, PHILADELPHIA, PENNSYLVANIA

Any dish calling for capon or capon breast can be done with a roasting chicken, which is far less expensive and easier to locate than capon.

2 capon breasts, 12 ounces each, skin left on but bone removed
Salt and freshly ground black pepper
2 sprigs fresh rosemary
2 slices (3 ounces each) fresh foie gras (see Mail Order Sources)
3 tablespoons olive oil
1 cup chicken stock

Preheat the oven to 500°F. Cut the capon breast in half. Make a slit almost all the way through each half breast to within ¼ inch of the edges to form a deep pocket, and turn the top half of the meat over without detaching it from the bottom layer. Sprinkle each breast lightly with salt and pepper.

Pull the leaves off both rosemary sprigs, discard the stems, and divide the leaves between the insides of each capon breast. Slice the foie gras into ½-inch slices and lay the slices down the middle of each capon breast. Reshape the breasts by folding them over the foie gras, and press the edges together to seal.

Heat 2 tablespoons of the olive oil over high heat in an oven-proof sauté pan or skillet. When the oil is hot and beginning to smoke, place the capon breasts in the pan, skin side down. Sear the capon for 2 to 3 minutes, or until golden brown. Turn the breasts over and place in the preheated oven for 20 minutes, or until both sides are golden and the breast is cooked through.

Remove the capon breasts from the oven and transfer to heated serving plates. Return the pan used to cook the capon to high heat and add the remaining oil. When the oil begins to sizzle, add the chicken stock and cook until reduced by three-quarters and syrupy, stirring up the browned bits from the bottom of the pan. Pour the sauce from the pan over the capon and serve.

NOTE: The capon breasts can be prepared for cooking up to 6 hours in advance and refrigerated, tightly covered.

SERVES 2 TO 4

STUFFED ROAST CAPON

ANDREA APUZZO, NEW ORLEANS, LOUISIANA

*While a capon would usually serve 6 people, this rich stuffing "stretches" the
bird to 8 portions. A roasting chicken can be used in place of the capon, or the
stuffing could also be placed under the skin of chicken parts such as breasts or
thighs.*

1 capon, approximately 5 pounds
$^1/_2$ pound chicken livers
$^1/_2$ pound pork loin, cubed
10 ounces bulk Italian sausage
2 ounces pancetta or bacon, roughly chopped
$^1/_2$ pound boneless chicken breast, skinned and roughly chopped
1 bunch Italian parsley, chopped
1 cup grated Parmesan cheese
1 medium onion, peeled and roughly chopped
1 garlic clove, peeled and minced
3 slices white bread, crusts removed
1 teaspoon chopped fresh marjoram
1 teaspoon chopped fresh rosemary
1 egg
$^1/_4$ cup brandy
2 tablespoons marsala wine
$^1/_3$ cup dry vermouth
Salt and freshly ground black pepper
$^1/_4$ cup olive oil

Rinse the capon under cold running water, and set aside. Combine the chicken livers, pork loin, sausage, pancetta, chicken breast, parsley, Parmesan, onion, garlic, bread, marjoram, and rosemary. Run the mixture through a food grinder or chop it in a food processor using on and off pulsing action, then add the egg, brandy, marsala, and vermouth. Season with salt and pepper. Fill the cavity of the capon with the stuffing and sew the opening closed, running the string through both legs.

Preheat the over to 400°F. Heat the olive oil in a roasting pan. Set the stuffed capon in the pan breast side up, cover the wing tips with foil, and roast for 30 minutes. Lower the temperature to 325°F. and roast for 2 hours, to an internal temperature of 180°F. when a thermometer is placed inside the stuffing. Baste with pan drippings every 15 minutes. Remove the capon from the oven, and allow to rest for 10 minutes before carving.

NOTE: The stuffing can be prepared up to 2 days in advance and refrigerated, tightly covered. Do not stuff the capon until just prior to roasting.

SERVES 8

CHEF'S TIP

Meat to be chopped with a food processor is easier to chop if the cubes of meat are less than 1 inch large and they have been chilled for 30 minutes in the freezer. Use on and off pulsing action, and do not crowd the work bowl too full.

ROAST DUCK WITH HUNTER'S SAUCE

RANDY BARLOW, NEW ORLEANS, LOUISIANA

This is an easy and delicious sauce for tender roast duck, and it goes well with a green vegetable such as Broccoli, Italian Style (page 166) and some polenta.

DUCK

2 ducks, 5 pounds each
6 celery stalks, chopped
2 medium onions, chopped
6 medium carrots, peeled and chopped
1 teaspoon dried oregano
1 teaspoon dried basil
Salt and freshly ground black pepper

SAUCE

¼ pound pancetta or bacon, chopped
1 large onion, peeled and chopped
½ pound shiitake, oyster, or other wild mushrooms or white culti-vated mushrooms, chopped
1 cup dry white wine
3 cups duck or chicken stock (pages 26–28)
1 cup diced tomatoes (page 30)
Salt and freshly ground black pepper

Preheat the oven to 300°F. Remove the neck and giblets from each duck. Loosely stuff the cavity of the ducks with celery, onions, carrots, oregano, basil, and salt and pepper, and place the remaining vegetables on the bottom of a roasting pan. Set the ducks on the vegetables. Bake for 3 to 4 hours, or until the skin is crisp and the legs move easily in their sockets. Let cool. Split the ducks in half and remove the vegetables and bones, reserving them to make stock, if you like.

To make the sauce, cook the pancetta or bacon until crisp in a large sauté pan or skillet. Remove from the pan with a slotted spoon, leaving the fat. Add the onion and cook over medium heat until translucent, about 3 minutes. Add the mushrooms and cook until browned, about 2 to 3 minutes. Add the white wine, stock, and tomatoes. Lower heat to medium-low and cook for 30 minutes, or until reduced by half. Season with salt and pepper. Serve each half duck with some of the sauce.

NOTE: The duck and sauce can be prepared up to 2 days in advance. Reheat the duck in a 300°F. oven for 15 to 20 minutes, or until hot, and reheat the sauce in a saucepan over low heat.

SERVES 4

CHEF'S TIP

While high in saturated fat, duck fat is excellent for frying potatoes and gives them an earthy taste. Save the fat rendered from duck dishes to use for that purpose, if you wish.

STUFFED LEG OF DUCK WITH RED WINE SAUCE

ROBERTO GEROMETTA, SAN FRANCISCO, CALIFORNIA

This is a hearty, wintery dish with a tasty stuffing filling a duck leg. Serve it with Baked Vegetables (page 161) and some Creamy Polenta (page 169).

DUCK AND SAUCE
1 whole duck, 4½ to 5 pounds, or 2 duck legs
6 tablespoons olive oil
1 onion, peeled and sliced
1 carrot, peeled and sliced
1 tomato, quartered
1 pinch thyme
1 bay leaf
6 black peppercorns
Salt
2 cups dry red wine
1 cup veal or duck stock

STUFFING
2 ounces pork
2 ounces pancetta or bacon
1 duck liver
2 tablespoons unsalted butter
1 shallot, chopped
1 egg yolk
2 tablespoons heavy cream
Salt and freshly ground black pepper

To make the sauce, cut the leg quarters off the duck, and remove the breast from the bone; reserve the legs for this dish and the remainder of the duck for another dish.

Chop the bones and place them in a heavy pan with the heated olive oil. Add the onion and carrot and brown. Add the quartered tomato, thyme, bay leaf, peppercorns, and salt. Deglaze with the red wine and veal stock, then cook approximately 1 hour. Strain the sauce and reserve.

To make the stuffing, put the pork, bacon, and duck liver through a meat grinder or chop them finely in a food processor using on and off pulsing action. In a sauté pan, heat the butter and sauté the shallot. Mix the chopped meats, shallot, egg yolk, cream, salt, and pepper in a bowl.

Preheat the oven to 450°F. Bone the duck legs and pound the meat flat between sheets of plastic wrap. Sprinkle the meat with salt and pepper. Place half the stuffing in the center of each leg. Close the leg over the stuffing and secure with toothpicks. Place the stuffed legs in a buttered pan and bake in the preheated oven for 20 to 25 minutes. Heat the reserved sauce, and adjust the seasoning.

To serve, slice the duck and place each portion on a pool of the sauce.

NOTE: The sauce and stuffing can be prepared 1 day in advance and refrigerated, tightly covered. Reheat the sauce over low heat and bring the stuffing to room temperature before stuffing the legs.

SERVES 2

CHEF'S TIP

Use a darning needle to prick the skin of a duck gently without piercing the meat, to rid the duck of excess fat while keeping the meat moist.

DUCK IN WINE SAUCE

UDO NECHUTNYS, ST. HELENA, CALIFORNIA

Rare duck breast is a treat, and the woodsy porcini mushrooms and red wine sauce enhance the gamy, tender meat. Serve this with Sautéed Vegetables (page 163) and some Creamy Polenta (page 169) or boiled pasta.

2 whole duck breasts, halved, with bone in (about 2 pounds each)
Salt and freshly ground black pepper
¹/₄ cup olive oil
¹/₄ pound (1 stick) unsalted butter
5 shallots, peeled and chopped
1 teaspoon peppercorns, cracked
2 ounces dried porcini mushrooms, soaked in boiling water for 10
   minutes, drained, and chopped
2 cups dry red wine
1 to 1¹/₂ cups duck stock or demi-glace (pages 12–13)
2 tomatoes, peeled, seeded, and chopped (page 30)

Preheat the oven to 450°F. Trim excess fat off the breasts, and season with salt and pepper. Heat the olive oil in a large sauté pan over medium-high heat. Gently prick the skin of the duck breasts, and place them skin side down in the hot pan for 3 minutes to melt their fat and brown the skin. Then place them in the oven to roast for 8 minutes, and set aside.

Melt the butter in a saucepan over medium heat, and add the shallots and peppercorns. Cook briefly. Add the porcini and wine, bring to a boil, and reduce slightly. Add the duck stock or demi-glace and the tomatoes and simmer for 30 minutes. Season with salt and pepper, and keep warm.

To serve, spoon the wine sauce onto warm plates. Trim the bone from the duck breasts, place each breast skin side down, and slice very thin. Fan the duck slices on top of the sauce.

NOTE: The sauce can be made up to 3 days in advance and refrigerated, tightly covered. Reheat it over low heat. The duck can be seared up to a few hours in advance, but should be roasted just prior to serving.

SERVES 4

DUCK STEW

LISA HANSON, NEW ORLEANS, LOUISIANA

Using olives as an enhancement is common in Italian cooking, and the salty flavor cuts the richness of this easy duck dish.

2 ducks, 5¹/₂ pounds each
Salt and freshly ground black pepper
4 tablespoons (¹/₂ stick) butter
2 cups diced onions
6 cups pitted and chopped black and green olives
4 cups peeled, seeded, and diced tomatoes (page 30)
1 cup port
¹/₃ cup duck fat or vegetable oil

Preheat the oven to 300°F. Season the ducks with salt and pepper to taste, and place them on a rack in a roasting pan. Roast for 3 to 4 hours, or until the legs move easily in their sockets. Remove from the oven, and when cool enough to handle, cut off the leg quarters, and pull the breast from the carcass.

In a large saucepan, melt the butter over medium heat and sauté the onions until translucent, about 3 minutes. Add the olives and tomatoes. Cook for 2 to 3 minutes. Add the port and cook for another 3 minutes. Keep warm.

In a large, deep sauté pan or skillet, heat the duck fat or vegetable oil over medium heat and sauté the duck breasts (skin side down) and legs until the duck skin is crisp.

To serve, pour the tomato and olive sauce on a serving platter. Slice the duck breast on the bias and fan the slices over the sauce. Set the duck legs on the side of the fanned breasts.

NOTE: The ducks can be roasted and the sauce can be made up to 2 days in advance and refrigerated, tightly covered. The duck will reheat in the pan while you reheat the sauce over low heat.

SERVES 4

ROASTED SQUAB WITH BACON AND SAGE

SYLVAIN PORTAY, NEW YORK, NEW YORK

This is a wonderful dish for a brisk, cold night, with the hearty flavor of the squab augmented by smoky bacon and aromatic sage.

SQUAB
4 large squab (see Mail Order Sources)
4 very thin slices bacon
4 large sage leaves
4 pieces (3 ounces each) fresh foie gras (see Mail Order Sources)

SAUCE
2 tablespoons unsalted butter
2 tablespoons olive oil
1 garlic clove, peeled and mashed
1 cup chicken stock
1 sprig fresh Italian parsley, coarsely chopped
1 small bunch fresh chives, finely chopped
5 leaves fresh basil, cut into julienne
1 small bunch fresh chervil, stemmed and coarsely chopped
1 tablespoon sherry vinegar

To prepare the squab, remove the legs and the backbone from each bird and reserve. Gently loosen the skin from the breast with one finger. Slide a thin slice of bacon and a sage leaf under the breast skin on each bird, then return the skin so that it covers the breast. Refrigerate until ready to cook.

To start the sauce, place a 7-inch sauté pan or skillet over medium-high heat and add the butter, 1 tablespoon of the olive oil, and the garlic. When the butter is very hot, add the squab legs and breast bones. Sear the bones for about 10 minutes, or until golden brown. Add the stock, and boil for 5 minutes, stirring to include the browned bits from the bottom of the pan. Strain and reserve the liquid, and set aside.

Put the remaining 1 tablespoon olive oil in a medium sauté pan or skillet and place over medium heat. Add the squab, skin side down, and cook for approximately 10 to 12 minutes, turning once to brown evenly.

To serve, remove the squab from the heat, and return the pan to the heat. Sear the foie gras about 30 seconds on each side, then sprinkle with salt and arrange on each of 4 warm plates. Pour off and discard the foie gras fat, and add the reserved stock mixture to the pan, scraping up any browned bits from the bottom. Add the parsley, chives, basil, chervil, and vinegar, and taste for seasoning. Adjust if necessary and pour the sauce over the squabs.

NOTE: The sauce can be started and the squab can be prepared up to cooking 1 day in advance and refrigerated, tightly covered.

SERVES 4

QUAIL STUFFED WITH PINE NUTS

HANS SCHADLER, WILLIAMSBURG, VIRGINIA

The quail are stuffed with a chicken mousse dotted with salty prosciutto, aromatic herbs, and crunchy pine nuts. The stuffing is delicious, and this dish can be served with any green vegetable and potatoes or pasta.

1/2 pound boneless chicken breast
1/2 teaspoon salt
1/2 teaspoon freshly ground white pepper
1/4 cup ice water
1/2 cup heavy cream
1/4 cup finely diced prosciutto
2 tablespoons pine nuts, toasted (pages 16–17)
2 tablespoons assorted fresh herbs (rosemary, parsley, thyme),
    finely chopped
4 semiboneless quail (see Mail Order Sources)
Salt and freshly ground black pepper
4 slices lean bacon
1/4 cup (1/2 stick) unsalted butter, melted

JODY ADAMS,
CHEF/OWNER, RIALTO, CAMBRIDGE, MA

Why did you become a chef?
I became a chef because I love food, I love to cook, I love restaurants, and it was the next step after being a line cook. I wanted to write my own menus and run my own kitchen.

How did you receive your training?
I trained while working with two wonderful and well-known chefs: Lydia Shire and Gordon Hammersley.

Any tips to pass on?
Taste everything and season each element of a dish before putting the elements together. Use the freshest, purest ingredients possible, and don't be afraid of fat; use it wisely.

To make the quail stuffing, remove and discard any skin or tissue from the chicken breast meat. Cut the chicken meat into 1-inch pieces and place them in the food processor. Add the salt and pepper and purée the chicken until smooth. Add the ice water and heavy cream and process until the chicken reaches a gummy consistency. Transfer the chicken purée to a chilled stainless steel bowl. Fold in the prosciutto, pine nuts, and herbs. Adjust the seasoning, and set aside.

To prepare the quail, rinse them under cold running water, pat them dry, and season them with salt and pepper. Fit a large pastry bag with a large plain tip, and fill the bag with the chicken mixture. Stuff the inside of the quail with the chicken purée and wrap each quail with a slice of bacon to close the cavity, securing the bacon with a toothpick. Brush the quail with the melted butter and set aside until needed.

Preheat the oven to 375°F. Roast the quail for 15 to 20 minutes, or until the birds are golden, the juices run clear, and an instant-read thermometer inserted into the center of the stuffing reads 175°F. Remove the quail from the oven and let rest for 5 minutes before serving.

NOTE: The quail stuffing can be prepared 1 day in advance, and refrigerated, tightly covered. Do not stuff the quail until just prior to serving.

SERVES 4

CHEF'S TIP

Save all the bits of skin and bone from trimming poultry in a bag in the freezer, and use them for making stock.

GRILLED MARINATED QUAIL

BRADLEY OGDEN, SAN FRANCISCO, CALIFORNIA

This is a very easy dish to make for an elegant party, and the combination of herbs, mustard, and wine for the marinade creates a complex flavor with little work. Be sure to note that the recipe must be started 2 days before serving.

8 semiboneless fresh quail (see Mail Order Sources)

MARINADE
¹/₂ cup brandy
1 tablespoon chopped fresh garlic
¹/₂ teaspoon cracked black pepper
3 tablespoons olive oil
¹/₄ cup Dijon mustard
¹/₂ cup Madeira
¹/₂ teaspoon kosher salt
12 sage leaves, chopped, or ¹/₂ teaspoon dried sage
8 rosemary sprigs, or 2 teaspoons dried rosemary
12 thyme sprigs, or ¹/₂ teaspoon dried thyme
8 savory sprigs, or ¹/₂ teaspoon dried savory

BASTING SAUCE
2 tablespoons olive oil
2 tablespoons stone-ground mustard
5 tablespoons unsalted butter, softened (¹/₂ stick plus 1 tablespoon)
2 teaspoons white wine vinegar
Salt and freshly ground black pepper

Cut the quail in half, rinse under cold running water, and pat dry. Combine all the marinade ingredients and marinate the quail halves in the refrigerator for 24 to 48 hours, turning occasionally.

Light a charcoal or gas grill. While the grill is heating, mix the olive oil, stone-ground mustard, soft butter, vinegar, and salt and pepper and set aside for basting.

Rub the grill with oil and place the quail on the hot grill, skin side down. Grill for 3 minutes, basting occasionally with basting sauce. Turn the halves and grill 3 minutes more, basting with the basting sauce. The quail should be medium-rare. Serve immediately.

NOTE: The quail have such a good flavor from the marinade that they will not suffer from being broiled rather than grilled.

SERVES 4

CHEF'S TIP

Kosher salt is a more coarsely ground salt than table salt. If you don't have kosher salt, use only half the amount of table salt to achieve the same degree of salinity.

STUFFED QUAIL WITH WILD MUSHROOM SAUCE

GERT RAUSCH, AUSTIN, TEXAS

Chicken livers add an earthy interest to the wild mushroom stuffing for quail, and the woodsy flavor of the mushrooms is intensified by the creamy sauce.

4 semiboneless quail (see Mail Order Sources)
Salt and freshly ground black pepper

STUFFING
4 tablespoons (¹/₂ stick) unsalted butter
¹/₃ cup finely chopped celery
¹/₄ cup finely chopped shallots
4 shiitake mushrooms, cleaned and diced
4 oyster mushrooms, cleaned and diced
4 button mushrooms, cleaned and diced
4 chicken livers, finely diced
³/₄ cup dry red wine
1¹/₂ cups crumbled corn bread
2 tablespoons chopped fresh basil
Salt and freshly ground black pepper

SAUCE
8 shiitake mushrooms, cleaned and diced
8 oyster mushrooms, cleaned and diced
8 morels, cleaned and sliced lengthwise
¹/₄ cup finely minced shallots
6 tablespoons (³/₄ stick) unsalted butter
¹/₂ cup dry red wine
2 cups veal or chicken stock (pages 26–28), or a combination of the two
1 cup heavy cream
Salt and freshly ground black pepper

Rinse the quail, pat dry, sprinkle with salt and pepper, and set aside.

To make the stuffing, heat the butter in a sauté pan or skillet over medium-high heat. Add the celery and shallots and sauté for 2 minutes, then add the 3 varieties of mushrooms and sauté until cooked, about 5 minutes. Add the diced chicken livers and sauté for 2 minutes, until they are firm but still rare. Add the red wine to the pan, simmering briefly to cook off the alcohol, then remove from the heat. Stir in the corn bread crumbs and basil, and season with salt and pepper to taste.

To make the sauce, sauté the 3 varieties of mushrooms and the shallots in the butter for 5 minutes over medium heat. Add the red wine, stock, and cream, and reduce by two-thirds, or until the mixture has thickened. Adjust the seasoning and set aside.

Preheat the oven to 450°F. Stuff the quail and secure the openings with toothpicks. Roast for 15 to 20 minutes, or until browned and cooked. Serve immediately.

NOTE: The stuffing and sauce can both be prepared up to 1 day in advance and refrigerated. Allow the stuffing to reach room temperature before stuffing the quail, and reheat the sauce over low heat.

SERVES 4

PHEASANT SAN XAVIER

MALTE BREITLOW, TUCSON, ARIZONA

Game birds and fruit are a traditional pairing, and the sauce for these succulent pheasant breasts is a vivid red from both the wine and the berries. Serve the dish with some wild rice and a green vegetable.

3 pheasant breasts (see Mail Order Sources)
3 tablespoons all-purpose flour
Salt and freshly ground black pepper
3 tablespoons clarified butter (page 11)
2 shallots, peeled and chopped
1 pint fresh raspberries (frozen unsweetened berries may be
    substituted)
1/2 cup Merlot or other full-bodied red wine
1 cup demi-glace (pages 12–13)
Whole raspberries and herb sprigs, such as thyme and rosemary,
    for garnish

Remove the skin from the pheasant breasts and pound them lightly to an even thickness. Dust them with flour and sprinkle with salt and pepper.

Heat the clarified butter in a sauté pan or skillet over high heat. When it is very hot, add the pheasant breasts and sauté until golden brown. Turn the breasts over, and add the shallots, raspberries, and Merlot. Stir, crushing the raspberries into the wine. Let simmer a few minutes, then add the demi-glace and simmer a few minutes longer. Add salt and pepper to taste, and serve, garnishing each plate with some whole raspberries and a sprig of fresh herb.

NOTE: The dish can be prepared up to 6 hours in advance and reheated over low heat.

SERVES 6 AS AN APPETIZER, 3 TO 4 AS AN ENTRÉE

MEAT AND GAME ENTRÉES FOR ALL SEASONS

Beef has not played as major a role in the Italian diet as it has in the American diet. Meat in general has been treated in Italy as a garnish more than the main attraction—a viewpoint now receiving favorable status here as well, as Americans try to cut back on the saturated fat in their diets. Lean, tender veal—from thinly pounded scaloppine to hearty braised shanks—is the meat favored not only by Italian chefs but by New American chefs as well. It is as delicate as chicken, and, except for braised dishes, it should be cooked quickly and gently to achieve the best flavor and texture. In addition to many veal recipes in this chapter, there are some wonderful treatments to add nuances of flavor to lusty, rich lamb as well as more traditional pork and beef.

ROASTED FREE-RANGE VEAL RACK WITH FRESH HERBS AND NATURAL JUICES

BERNARD DERVIEUX, ASPEN, COLORADO

This is an incredibly elegant dish for a dinner party, served with Herbed Boiled Potatoes (page 173) and Baked Vegetables (page 161). The veal is delicate, and the fresh herbs enhance its flavor. Use the same marinade for veal chops, grilling or broiling them.

1 whole rack of veal (7 chops)
¼ cup chopped fresh oregano
¼ cup chopped fresh thyme
¼ cup chopped fresh tarragon
¼ cup chopped fresh rosemary
¼ cup chopped fresh chervil
1¼ cups olive oil
2 garlic cloves, peeled and chopped
4 tablespoons (½ stick) unsalted butter
Salt and freshly ground black pepper
2 cups veal stock, preferably homemade (pages 26–28)

To prepare the veal, trim away the bones encasing the eye of the veal rack and scrape the meat from the ends of the rib bones. Using cotton string, tie the rack between the bones to keep the meat in a cylindrical shape, and tie the roast together.

Chop all the herbs and mix half of the mixture with 1 cup of the olive oil and the garlic. Rub the mixture over all surfaces of the veal and marinate at room temperature for 2 hours, or in the refrigerator, covered with plastic wrap, overnight.

Preheat the oven to 400°F. Heat the remaining $1/4$ cup olive oil and 2 tablespoons of the butter in a roasting pan large enough to hold the veal, and when it is hot and the butter foam has started to subside, sear the veal and brown it on all sides.

Sprinkle the veal with salt and pepper. Roast the veal for 35 to 45 minutes, turning it over once halfway through the roasting.

Remove the veal to a heated platter and allow it to rest for 10 minutes. Pour off the grease and deglaze the pan with the veal stock, boiling until reduced by half. Add the remaining fresh herbs, season with salt and pepper to taste, and whisk in the remaining 2 tablespoons of butter.

To serve, carve the rack into chops and place on a bed of the sauce. Pass extra sauce separately.

NOTE: The dish must be cooked just prior to serving.

SERVES 6

SAUTÉED VEAL CHOPS

HALEY GABEL, NEW ORLEANS, LOUISIANA

If you don't have a ribbed skillet or stovetop grill to give these chops grill marks, just sear them in a regular skillet. The same treatment works as well with the same timing if using chicken breasts that have been boned but not skinned. This combination of veal chops with a rich, savory sauce, paired with quickly cooked Sautéed Escarole (page 167), is an elegant dish for fall and winter.

4 veal chops
Olive oil for coating
Salt and freshly ground black pepper
4 sprigs fresh sage

SAUCE
1 tablespoon unsalted butter
1 tablespoon minced chicken livers
Pinch of dried red pepper flakes
2 tablespoons balsamic vinegar
2 teaspoons chopped fresh sage
1¹/₂ cups veal stock or chicken stock, reduced by one-half
Pinch of salt

Preheat the oven to 400°F. Coat each chop with olive oil and season on both sides with salt and pepper. Heat a ribbed skillet until very hot, or use a stovetop grill. Place the sage sprigs on the grill. Place each chop over a sage sprig and sear the chops for a minute or so on each side to make grill marks. Put the chops in a large ovenproof skillet and bake for about 8 minutes for medium-rare.

To make the sauce, melt the butter in a medium sauté pan and sauté the chicken livers and red pepper flakes for about 2 minutes. Pour in the balsamic vinegar and stir over medium heat, scraping the browned bits from the bottom of the pan. Add the sage and stock. Cook for about 4 to 5 minutes over medium heat to reduce. Season with salt.

To serve, place a veal chop on each plate, and surround it with the sauce.

SERVES 4

VEAL PICCATA

GOFFREDO FRACCARO, NEW ORLEANS, LOUISIANA

Piccata is a term used in Italian cooking for dishes given a tangy flavor with lemon juice. This is a classic from the Italian-American repertoire.

12 veal scallops, about 2 ounces each
Salt and freshly ground black pepper
All-purpose flour for dredging
¼ cup olive oil
2 tablespoons beef stock, heated
Juice of 1 lemon
6 tablespoons (¾ stick) unsalted butter
2 tablespoons minced fresh parsley

Gently pound the scallops until thin and flat, but not broken. Sprinkle them with salt and pepper. Dredge lightly in flour.

Heat the olive oil in a large sauté pan over high heat. Add the veal, and fry for about 45 seconds per side; this may have to be done in batches. Remove the veal from the pan and keep warm.

Drain off the fat and add the stock, lemon juice, butter, and parsley. Stir well and heat the sauce thoroughly. Spoon the sauce over the veal scallops and serve immediately.

NOTE: This dish must be cooked just prior to serving; however the ingredients can be prepared for cooking a few hours in advance.

SERVES 6

BRAISED VEAL SHANKS

MICHAEL FOLEY, CHICAGO, ILLINOIS

The fresh taste of ginger is what transforms this otherwise classic ossobuco into an Italian-inspired dish. Serve this with Wild Mushroom Risotto (page 78) or some orzo and a green salad.

4 tablespoons (¹/₂ stick) clarified butter (page 11)
¹/₄ cup olive oil
Salt and freshly ground black pepper
4 center-cut veal shanks, each 1 inch thick, at room temperature
2 onions, peeled and chopped
1 stalk celery, chopped
2 carrots, peeled and chopped
3 garlic cloves, peeled and minced
1 tablespoon tomato paste
1 pinch dried thyme
1 bay leaf
2 tablespoons minced fresh parsley
¹/₂ teaspoon peppercorns
4 cups chicken stock, preferably homemade (pages 26–28)
1 cup veal stock
1 tomato, peeled, seeded, and chopped (page 30)
2 tablespoons minced fresh ginger
2 leaves fresh basil, julienned

Heat a large, deep ovenproof sauté pan. Add the clarified butter and olive oil. When they are hot, salt the shanks and put them in the pan to brown. Add the chopped onion, celery, carrots, garlic, and tomato paste. Add the thyme, bay leaf, parsley, and peppercorns. When the meat is brown on both sides, remove it from the pan and reserve in a warm place.

Preheat the oven to 350°F. Add the chicken and veal stocks to the ovenproof sauté pan. Bring the stocks to a boil and reduce by one-third. Put the shanks back into the pan and add the chopped tomato and ginger. Place the pan in the oven and roast the shanks for 45 minutes. Turn the shanks and roast until the meat is tender, approximately 45 minutes longer. Remove the shanks from the pan and reserve in a warm place, covered. Over high heat reduce the roasting juices to 2 cups. Add the fresh basil. Purée all the vegetables and herbs with the juices through a food mill. Return to the pan and reduce again if necessary. Season with salt and pepper, and serve immediately.

NOTE: The dish is better if prepared a day in advance and reheated over low heat, covered.

SERVES 4

CHEF'S TIP

When you prepare any meat (or poultry) dish in advance, remove and discard the solid layer of fat that forms on the top when it chills.

OSSOBUCO

BOB ROTH, NEW ORLEANS, LOUISIANA

Ossobuco, braised veal shank, is an Italian dish traditionally served with risotto. This particular sauce is velvety smooth, and makes enough for a few batches, so the sauce can be frozen, so the dish is even easier to make the second time.

4 bacon slices, chopped
1 pound onions, peeled and cut into large dice
3 carrots, peeled and cut into ¹/₂-inch pieces
1 garlic clove, peeled and minced
2 tablespoons tomato paste
1 tablespoon all-purpose flour
4 cups dry red wine
4 cups chicken stock or broth, preferably homemade (pages 26–28)
4 cups beef stock or broth, preferably homemade (pages 26–28)
2 tablespoons brandy
2 teaspoons cornstarch
1 tablespoon unsalted butter
Salt and freshly ground black pepper
1 tablespoon vegetable oil
4 center-cut veal shanks, each 2 inches thick

In a large, deep casserole suitable for direct heat, cook the bacon until crisp and remove the bacon to drain on paper towels. Sauté the onions, carrots, and garlic in the bacon fat until browned, about 10 minutes. Add the tomato paste and cook over low heat, stirring occasionally, for 5 minutes. Stir in the flour and cook over low heat, stirring constantly, for 5 minutes. Add the red wine, and cook over low heat for 30 minutes, or until reduced by half, stirring constantly near the end of the cooking time. Add the chicken and veal stocks or broth and simmer for 45 minutes. Remove from the heat and strain through a fine-meshed sieve. Mix the brandy and cornstarch together thoroughly. Add to the sauce, stirring until the sauce is thickened and smooth. Stir in the butter.

Preheat the oven to 375°F. Season with salt and pepper and oil the veal shanks. Place the shanks in an ovenproof casserole and bake for 15 to 20 minutes, or until lightly browned. Add to the sauce and cook, partially covered, over low heat for 2 hours, or until fork-tender.

NOTE: The dish is even better if prepared up to 2 days in advance and reheated in a 350°F. oven until hot.

SERVES 4

CHEF'S TIP

Veal shanks will keep their round shape if tied with kitchen string before braising; however they may take longer to cook, since the meat fibers are condensed.

VEAL TENDERLOIN CRUSTED WITH FRESH HERBS AND BLACK PEPPER

MICHAEL UDDO, NEW ORLEANS, LOUISIANA

If you are a fan of steak au poivre, you'll be an instant convert to this veal dish, which is coated with a mixture of minced herbs, coarsely ground black pepper, and Dijon mustard. Chef Uddo serves his veal tenderloin with Smoked Tomato and Shiitake Mushroom Risotto (page 80).

2 tablespoons minced fresh dill
2 tablespoons minced fresh parsley
2 tablespoons minced fresh rosemary
1½ tablespoons minced chives
¼ cup coarsely ground black pepper
¼ cup Dijon mustard
2 tablespoons dry white wine
Salt
One 12-ounce veal tenderloin, trimmed
2 tablespoons olive oil
1 cup demi-glace (pages 12–13)
2 tablespoons port wine

FRANCESCO ANTONUCCI, CHEF AND OWNER, REMI, NEW YORK, NY

Why did you become a chef?
My family was in the food business. I love food and working with food. I thought being a chef would be a great way to travel and experience different things.

How did you receive your training?
I attended the Culinary Institute in Venice. However, I gained most of my cooking skills by experimenting in my own kitchen.

Any tips to pass along?
The most important utensil to have in the kitchen is a great knife.

To make the herb crust, combine the dill, parsley, rosemary, chives, and pepper in a small bowl. In a separate cup, stir the mustard and wine together until well blended. Set aside.

To prepare the veal, preheat the oven to 450°F. Lightly salt the veal tenderloin. Heat the olive oil to very hot in a large ovenproof skillet and brown the veal on all sides. Bake for about 20 minutes for medium-rare. Leave the oven on. Remove the meat from the skillet. With a small spoon, coat the veal thoroughly with the mustard mixture, then coat it heavily all over with the herb mixture. Return the veal to the skillet and bake for 1½ minutes. Do not brown the herbs. Remove from the oven and let rest.

Combine the demi-glace and port in a small saucepan and bring to a boil over medium heat. Lower the heat and simmer for 5 minutes.

To serve, slice the tenderloin on the diagonal, and divide among 4 serving plates, then drizzle with the port wine demi-glace sauce.

NOTE: While the dish must be prepared at the last minute, the sauce can be made up to 2 days in advance and refrigerated, tightly covered. Reheat over low heat.

SERVES 4

CHEF'S TIP

The easiest way to get coarsely ground black pepper is to place the whole peppercorns in a heavy resealable plastic bag and pound the bag with the bottom of a small, heavy skillet until the right texture is reached.

VEAL WITH WILD MUSHROOMS

GERHARD BRILL, ORANGE BEACH, ALABAMA

This is a great dish for when you have more money than time to prepare a dinner. The ingredients are expensive, but the veal comes to the table in a matter of minutes. Serve it with noodles or wild rice.

8 veal cutlets, 3 ounces each
1 teaspoon salt
$^1/_2$ teaspoon freshly ground black pepper
$^1/_2$ teaspoon cayenne pepper
$^1/_2$ teaspoon cumin
All-purpose flour for dredging
3 tablespoons unsalted butter
$^1/_4$ cup chopped shallots
2 ounces morel mushrooms, sliced
2 ounces cèpes mushrooms, sliced
2 ounces chanterelle mushrooms, sliced
1 ounce cultivated white mushrooms, sliced
2 tablespoons brandy
$^1/_4$ cup red wine
$^3/_4$ cup demi-glace (pages 12–13)
Salt and freshly ground black pepper

Place the veal cutlets between two sheets of plastic wrap and pound to an even thickness of ¼ inch with the flat side of a meat mallet or the bottom of a heavy skillet. Combine the salt, peppers, and cumin, and sprinkle over the cutlets.

Dredge the cutlets lightly in flour, shaking off any excess. Melt the butter in a large skillet over medium-high heat and sauté the veal cutlets until brown, about 1 minute per side. Remove the veal from the pan and add the shallots and morel, cèpes, chanterelle, and cultivated mushrooms. Sauté for 3 to 4 minutes, or until the mushrooms are cooked, stirring constantly. Add the brandy to the pan, and, tilting the pan away from your face, light the brandy with a long kitchen match. Shake the pan until the flames die down. Add the red wine, demi-glace, salt, and pepper, and bring to a boil. Return the veal to the pan, and cook for 2 minutes.

To serve, place the veal cutlets on warm serving plates. Simmer the sauce for another minute, then ladle over the veal.

NOTE: The dish can be prepared up to 6 hours in advance and reheated over a low flame.

SERVES 4

VEAL ADRIANA

ADRIANA GIRAMONTI, MILL VALLEY, CALIFORNIA

Delicate veal scaloppine are sauced with a tangy mustard cream sauce in this quick dish. Thinly pounded chicken breasts will work as well as veal; sauté them for a few minutes longer, however.

2 tablespoons Dijon mustard
Juice of 1 lemon
³/₄ cup heavy cream
1 pound veal scaloppine, pounded thin
Salt and freshly ground white pepper
All-purpose flour for dredging
¹/₃ cup olive oil
1 cup white wine
¹/₄ cup chicken broth
¹/₄ cup demi-glace (pages 12–13)
1 tablespoon minced fresh parsley

Mix the mustard with the lemon juice and cream, and set aside.

Sprinkle the veal with salt and pepper and lightly dust with flour, shaking off any excess. In a sauté pan, heat the olive oil over medium-high heat. Sauté the veal for 1 minute on each side; this may have to be done in batches. Discard the oil and add the wine to the pan. Bring the liquid to a boil, then lower the heat and add the chicken broth, demi-glace, parsley, and reserved mustard sauce. Simmer for 3 or 4 minutes, or until slightly thickened. Return the veal to the pan to heat, and serve immediately.

NOTE: The dish can be prepared up to a few hours in advance. Reheat the sauce first to a simmer and then add the veal to heat through.

SERVES 4

GRILLED VEAL CHOPS

BILLY VALENTINE, EAST HAMPTON, NEW YORK

The combination of garlic and rosemary is stunning with delicate veal, and the simple paste creates a wonderful coating on the chops. Serve these with caponata and some garlic bread.

2 tablespoons crushed garlic
2 teaspoons crushed fresh rosemary
¹/₂ teaspoon freshly ground black pepper
¹/₂ teaspoon salt
4 veal chops, 10 ounces each
Caponata (page 158)

In a small bowl, blend the garlic, rosemary, pepper, and salt into a paste. Rub the paste into the veal chops and let them rest at room temperature for 2 hours.

Light a charcoal or gas grill. Sear the veal over hot coals for 3 to 4 minutes per side. Move them closer to the edge of the grill and cook for 2 minutes on each side or until medium-rare.

To serve, place a chop on each of 4 warm serving plates. Serve with caponata and garlic bread.

NOTE: The chops can also be baked in a 375°F. oven for 15 minutes; turn once.

SERVES 4

CHEF'S TIP

Herbs such as rosemary and parsley can be frozen, wrapped tightly in plastic wrap. Freeze whole parsley sprigs, and strip the leaves from the woody stems of rosemary. Once frozen, the herbs can be chopped by hitting the plastic wrap with the blunt side of a knife.

GRILLED VEAL TENDERLOIN

MICHAEL FOLEY, CHICAGO, ILLINOIS

Tender veal tenderloin is frequently difficult to find, but this same treatment will work well with veal loin chops. The subtle herb oil enhances the delicacy of the veal, and it is very easy to make.

8 veal tenderloin pieces, 2 ounces each
Salt and freshly ground black pepper
2 tablespoons olive oil
1/2 teaspoon dried basil
1 bay leaf, broken into pieces
1/2 teaspoon dried thyme
1/2 teaspoon minced oregano
1 teaspoon minced fresh parsley

Place the tenderloin pieces between 2 sheets of plastic wrap and pound gently to form medallions from the long cylinders by pressing them flatter, so they look similar to filets mignons from beef tenderloin.

Season the tenderloin pieces with salt and pepper. Combine the olive oil with the basil, bay leaf, thyme, oregano, and parsley to make an herb oil. Coat the tenderloins with the herb oil, and marinate at room temperature for at least 1 hour.

Light a charcoal or gas grill, or preheat an oven broiler. Grill the tenderloin pieces for about 10 minutes, to medium-rare or medium, according to preference. Serve immediately.

NOTE: The veal can be marinated in the refrigerator overnight. Grill just prior to serving.

SERVES 4

OVEN-ROASTED PORK AND RABBIT

FRANCESCO RICCHI, WASHINGTON, DC

The flavor and texture of pork and rabbit make an excellent combination when infused with garlic and rosemary; however, one could use pork alone in a larger quantity and still have an excellent dish.

2½ pounds boneless pork loin
4 sprigs fresh rosemary
4 garlic cloves, peeled and thinly sliced
Salt and freshly ground black pepper
½ cup (1 stick) unsalted butter
1 fresh rabbit (about 3 pounds)
¾ cup olive oil
2 cups red wine

Trim the pork loin of excess fat, slice it almost in half lengthwise, and set aside. Finely chop the rosemary and the garlic together and season with salt and pepper. With a sharp knife, make 5 cuts, 1½ to 2 inches deep, around the pork loin, evenly spaced. Place ½ teaspoon of the garlic-rosemary mixture in each pocket, then tuck ½ teaspoon butter over the herbs. Sprinkle the inside of the loin with the herb mixture and dot with 2½ tablespoons butter. Roll the loin up with some of the herbs on the inside, then tie the roast closed with kitchen twine at 1-inch intervals.

Trim the rabbit of any excess fat and place the carcass on its back. Pull one leg away from the body, then use a sharp knife to cut through the meat and the joint to separate the leg from the loin. Repeat with the other leg. Locate the breastbone, then use a heavy knife to split and remove it. Run your finger down the rabbit's rib cage to locate the backbone. Use the tip of the knife to scrape each rib bone away from the meat along one side, stopping when you reach the thin skin at the base of the backbone. Repeat with the other side of the rabbit and remove the backbone.

(continued on next page)

Preheat the oven to 400°F. Season the inside of the rabbit with the herb mixture. Top with 1½ tablespoons butter and fold the rabbit's skin like a package. Tie the rabbit, using the same method as for the pork loin. Puncture the reserved legs at 1-inch intervals and stuff each one with part of the remaining herb mixture and 1 teaspoon of butter for each leg.

Place the pork and the rabbit in a large roasting pan and sprinkle them with any remaining herbs. Drizzle the roasts with olive oil and roast in the preheated oven for 40 to 50 minutes, turning the meat regularly to ensure even browning. At this point the pork should register 155°F. on an instant-read meat thermometer.

Remove the pan from the oven and place it on the stove over medium-high heat. Add the wine to the pan, stirring to dislodge the browned bits on the bottom of the pan. (Continue to turn the roasts while the wine is reducing.) When the wine has reduced by two-thirds and has a syrupy consistency, remove the meat and transfer it to a serving platter. Slice the roasted pork and rabbit, and serve with the roasting juices and wine reduction.

NOTE: The meats can be prepared for roasting up to 1 day in advance and refrigerated, tightly covered. Allow the meat to stand at room temperature for 30 minutes before roasting.

SERVES 8

MEDALLIONS OF PORK

Warren Le Ruth, Bay St. Louis, Mississippi

Topping meats with sauce and cheese is part of the Italian-American tradition. In this dish, the mustard adds a sharp flavor to contrast with the cheese.

4 pork medallions (2 ounces each) from the tenderloin or loin
2 teaspoons Dijon mustard
1 tablespoon all-purpose flour
$\frac{1}{4}$ teaspoon salt
1 pinch white pepper
1 tablespoon vegetable oil
1 tablespoon unsalted butter
1 cucumber, peeled, seeded, and sliced in 1-inch pieces
4 slices ($\frac{1}{2}$ ounce each) fontina cheese
1 cup dry white wine
1 teaspoon chopped parsley

Pound the pork until thin and spread each with one-quarter of the mustard. Mix the flour with the salt and pepper and sprinkle them on the meat. Heat the vegetable oil and butter in a large sauté pan or skillet over medium-high heat until quite hot. Add the pork, mustard side up. Turn every 30 seconds or so for 2 minutes. Remove to a hot plate to keep warm.

Add the cucumber and remaining mustard. Stir and toss to coat with the oil, butter, and mustard for 2 minutes. Push the cucumber slices to one side of the pan. Return the pork to the pan and cover with cheese. Distribute the cucumbers around the pork, pour on half ($\frac{1}{2}$ cup) of the wine, and cover the pan for 1 minute. Remove the cover, add the remaining $\frac{1}{2}$ cup wine, and cover for another minute, or until the cheese begins to melt. Sprinkle with chopped parsley and serve.

NOTE: The dish can be prepared up to 2 hours in advance and kept in the pan. Reheat briefly before serving.

SERVES 2

ROASTED SAUSAGES AND GRAPES

GEORGE GERMON, PROVIDENCE, RHODE ISLAND

Just as salty prosciutto and succulent figs are a natural flavor combination, so are tangy grapes and zesty sausages. You can vary the type of sausage depending on taste, but the fennel and garlic in Italian sausages are a necessary part of the dish. The chef serves this on mashed potatoes; just use your favorite recipe.

1½ pounds hot Italian sausage, cut into 3-inch lengths
1½ pounds sweet Italian sausage, cut into 3-inch lengths
3 tablespoons unsalted butter
6 to 7 cups (2½ pounds) red or green seedless grapes, stems
   removed
¼ cup balsamic vinegar

MICHAEL UDDO,
CHEF, COURTYARD GRILL, NEW ORLEANS, LA

Why did you become a chef?
I was raised around great food. I'm a third-generation Sicilian, and my grandparents came to America with simple ideas that eventually grew into Progresso Foods. It has always been my appreciation for the meal in front of me and the cook who prepared it.

How did you receive your training?
My training started at the age of twelve in a family-owned restaurant, where I worked my way up from being a dishwasher to the cooking line. I then trained at Cordon Bleu in London and apprenticed with two three-star Michelin chefs in that city before I returned to New Orleans to train in some of the city's best restaurants.

Any tips to pass on?
Don't make every recipe you see in a cookbook verbatim. Remember, it's just a recipe, and it's open to your interpretation and the way you enjoy doing it. Also, you never grow old at the dinner table.

Preheat the oven to 500°F. Bring a large pot of water to a boil over high heat. Prick the sausages with the tip of a knife or a metal skewer and put them in the boiling water. Boil the sausages gently for 8 minutes, then drain them and reserve.

Melt the butter in a large flameproof roasting pan over low heat. Add the grapes to the pan and toss to coat them with the butter. With tongs, transfer the parboiled sausages to the roasting pan and push them down into the grapes so the sausages will not brown too quickly.

Place the pan in the preheated oven and roast the sausages and grapes, turning the sausages once, until the grapes are soft and the sausages have browned, 20 to 25 minutes. With a slotted spoon, transfer the sausages and grapes to a heated serving platter.

Place the roasting pan on top of the stove over a medium-high flame and add the balsamic vinegar. Scrape up any browned bits on the bottom of the roasting pan and allow the vinegar and juices to reduce until they are thick and syrupy.

Pour the sauce over the sausages and grapes and serve immediately, accompanied by mashed potatoes.

NOTE: The dish can be prepared up to 2 days in advance and refrigerated, tightly covered. Reheat it in a 350°F. oven, covered, for 15 minutes, or until hot.

SERVES 6 TO 8

CHEF'S TIP

Look for full plump grape bunches that are still firmly attached to pliable stems that snap back when you let them go. Avoid grapes with wrinkled skin, sticky grapes, or brittle stems; these are all signs that the grapes are not fresh.

LOIN OF LAMB WITH GARLIC SAUCE

John Neal, New Orleans, Louisiana

The garlicky sauce with a touch of anchovy is a robust treatment for lusty lamb, and the dish is elegant and easy, if not exactly economical. The chef serves this with Baked Vegetables (page 161) in the center of the plate.

4 lamb loins, 5 ounces each
Salt and freshly ground black pepper
2 tablespoons minced fresh thyme
¼ cup peanut oil

SAUCE
¼ cup garlic vinegar
2 tablespoons puréed roasted garlic (pages 13–14)
2 tablespoons minced fresh thyme
1 cup dry white wine
1½ cups demi-glace (pages 12–13) or reduced-salt beef stock
    reduced by half
1 tablespoon anchovy paste
1 tablespoon unsalted butter
Dash of lemon juice
Salt and freshly ground black pepper

Preheat the over to 375°F. Season the lamb with salt, pepper, and thyme. In a large sauté pan or skillet, heat the peanut oil and sear the lamb on both sides for a total of 2 minutes. Bake for 15 minutes for medium-rare.

To make the garlic sauce, combine the garlic vinegar, roasted garlic, thyme, and white wine in a medium saucepan. Cook over medium heat until reduced by two-thirds, about 5 minutes. Add the demi-glace or stock and cook again to reduce by two-thirds or until thickened, about 4 to 5 minutes. Whisk in the anchovy paste, butter, lemon juice, and salt and pepper to taste.

To serve, slice the lamb and fan the slices. Nap with garlic sauce.

NOTE: The sauce can be made up to 2 days in advance and refrigerated, tightly covered. Reheat over low heat until hot.

SERVES 4

CHEF'S TIP

One tablespoon of anchovy paste is the equivalent of 5 anchovy fillets ground with some of the oil from the can. So if you don't have paste, you can make your own.

MARINATED LAMB MEDALLIONS

PAUL INGENITO, NEW YORK, NEW YORK

This simple and flavorful marinated grilled lamb is a perfect entrée to serve with Fried Eggplant (page 164) and a loaf of crusty bread for a fine dinner. The lamb must be marinated for 8 hours.

1 loin of lamb (or boned leg), approximately 2 pounds of
    boneless meat
1 cup olive oil
1 cup finely chopped onion
2 tablespoons fresh lemon juice
1 tablespoon minced garlic
2 tablespoons fresh minced parsley
1 teaspoon salt
1 teaspoon freshly ground black pepper

ANDRÉ POIROT,
EXECUTIVE CHEF, THE ROYAL SONESTA HOTEL,
NEW ORLEANS, LA

Why did you become a chef?
I have always been drawn to food, and I had to help around the house, since my mother had to support a family of five children. I started by baking cakes, and when it came time to choose a career, I did not have to look far to know what I wanted to do with my life.

How did you receive your training?
I trained in France, starting when I was fourteen years old in a small hotel to make pocket money. I then spent two years at culinary college, where I graduated with honors.

Any tips to pass on?
When reheating a thick soup or sauce, there is a good chance that it will scorch before it comes to a boil. To avoid this, add 1/4 inch of water to the pot before adding the soup and this will discourage

Trim the lamb of all fat, and cut the meat into 4 even pieces. Combine the remaining ingredients in a stainless steel or glass bowl and mix thoroughly. Place the 4 pieces of lamb loin into the marinade and toss to coat evenly. Cover and refrigerate for 8 hours or overnight, turning occasionally for thorough marination. Drain and reserve the marinade.

Light a charcoal or gas grill. When the coals are medium-hot and lightly covered with gray ash, place the lamb sections approximately 4 inches above the coals. Grill the lamb uncovered for approximately 4 to 5 minutes per side for rare, 5 to 7 minutes for medium, and 8 to 10 minutes for well done. Baste the lamb with the reserved marinade as it grills, and remove it from the grill with tongs to a warm platter. Allow it to rest for 10 minutes before carving.

To serve, slice each section of lamb into 3 pieces and arrange in a triangular pattern on the plates.

NOTE: The lamb can marinate for up to 24 hours before grilling, and once grilled it can be served at room temperature as well as warm.

SERVES 4

CHEF'S TIP

Lemon juice and other acidic foods added to a marinade will tenderize meat; however do not exceed the amount in a recipe, or the meat will "cook" from the acidulation and turn gray.

PEPPERED BEEF TENDERLOIN WITH BAROLO SAUCE

HANS SCHADLER, WILLIAMSBURG, VIRGINIA

While the cranberries are an American addition, beef with peppercorns in a rich red wine sauce is as much a part of the Italian repertoire as it is the French.

4 beef tenderloin steaks (preferably tail pieces), 2 ounces each
$^1/_4$ cup olive oil
$^1/_4$ cup Dijon mustard
$^1/_4$ cup mixed peppercorns (green, black, white, and pink), crushed
  with a rolling pin or coarsely cracked in a grinder

SAUCE
1 tablespoon olive oil
1 shallot, peeled and finely chopped
2 garlic cloves, peeled and finely chopped
$^1/_2$ cup Barolo, or other dry red wine
1 cup veal or beef stock
Salt and freshly ground black pepper
Cayenne pepper
$^1/_4$ cup dried cranberries

To prepare the tenderloin, brush the beef with the olive oil and mustard, then roll each piece in the cracked peppercorns. Set aside until ready to cook.

To make the sauce, heat the olive oil in an 8-inch sauté pan or skillet over medium heat. Add the shallots and garlic and sauté, stirring frequently, until the shallots are translucent, about 3 minutes. Add the red wine, bring to a boil, and let the liquid reduce in volume by one-half. Add the stock, then reduce by half again, or until the sauce is thick enough to coat the back of a spoon. Adjust the seasonings with salt, pepper, and cayenne. Add the cranberries, remove from heat, and set aside.

Preheat the oven to 350°F. Heat a 12-inch nonstick sauté pan or skillet over high heat, and sear the tenderloins to seal, about 2 minutes on each side. (Turn the tenderloins to brown them evenly.) Transfer the tenderloins to a shallow roasting pan. Roast the beef in the oven for 6 to 10 minutes, or to the degree of doneness desired. Remove the beef from the oven and let rest for 5 minutes before serving.

To serve, reheat the sauce and spoon it on top of the beef.

NOTE: The sauce can be made up to 2 days in advance and refrigerated, tightly covered. Reheat it slowly over low heat while the beef is cooking.

SERVES 4

SADDLE OF RABBIT WITH ROSEMARY

MAX SCHACHER, SAN FRANCISCO, CALIFORNIA

Delicate rabbit is marinated with aromatic rosemary, then roasted, and sauced simply with the same flavors. Serve this with some crispy potatoes and a mild vegetable like zucchini. (Note that the rabbit must marinate 24 to 48 hours.)

1 saddle section from a 3-pound rabbit
1¹/₂ cups white wine
3 sprigs fresh rosemary
1 small carrot, peeled and chopped
¹/₂ medium onion, peeled and chopped
1 stalk celery, chopped
1 garlic clove, peeled and crushed
Salt and freshly ground black pepper
2 tablespoons unsalted butter
1 tablespoon olive oil
1 cup rabbit or chicken stock
1 tomato, sliced

Put the saddle of rabbit in a small bowl with 1 cup of the white wine, 1 sprig rosemary, the carrot, onion, celery, and garlic. Cover the bowl with plastic wrap and refrigerate for 24 to 48 hours.

Remove the rabbit from the marinade and dry with paper towels; reserve the marinade. Salt and pepper the rabbit and pre-heat the oven to 450°F. Put 1 tablespoon of the butter and the olive oil in a medium roasting pan. Heat until the butter sizzles. Place the rabbit in the pan, skin side up, and brown. Turn, wrapping the flaps around the fillet to protect it, and cook until light brown. Place the pan in the oven and roast for 10 minutes, until medium-rare, basting often.

Add the vegetables from the marinade to the pan with the rabbit and cook for another 5 minutes, basting and turning occasionally. Remove the rabbit from the pan and keep warm. Trim the saddle flaps from the rabbit, chop them coarsely, and return them to the pan with the vegetables. On the stove top, sauté briefly and skim the fat. Deglaze the pan with the remaining 1/2 cup wine, add the stock, and reduce by one-half. Add the tomato and sauté while stirring. Strain through a sieve, reserving the liquid (for sauce) and discarding the vegetables. Add the remaining 1 tablespoon butter to the liquid and whisk until smooth.

Remove the fillet of rabbit from the saddle. Cut the saddle bone crosswise and place one section on each of 2 plates. Cut the fillet of rabbit into very thin slices lengthwise. Cover with sauce, and garnish with sprigs of rosemary. Serve immediately.

NOTE: The dish can be prepared a few hours in advance. Reheat the rabbit in the sauce before carving.

SERVES 2

CHEF'S TIP

Any dish calling for rabbit can also be made with chicken parts.

RABBIT IN WINE SAUCE

GERARD CROZIER, NEW ORLEANS, LOUISIANA

While the French use bay leaves as an accent flavor, the Italians love its robust taste, which works very well in this dish. An easy way to slice mushrooms so they are of uniform size is with a hard-boiled egg slicer. Serve it with some pasta to go under the sauce, and a green salad.

2 rabbits, cut into serving pieces
$^1/_2$ cup plus 2 tablespoons all-purpose flour
Salt and freshly ground black pepper
$^1/_4$ cup vegetable oil
$^1/_4$ cup chopped onions
1 pound mushrooms, cleaned and sliced
2 tomatoes, peeled, seeded, and chopped (page 30)
3 bay leaves
1 tablespoon tomato paste
2 cups white wine
2 tablespoons unsalted butter, softened

Preheat the oven to 350°F. Sprinkle the rabbit pieces with $^1/_2$ cup of the flour, salt, and pepper, and dust evenly, shaking to remove any excess. Heat the vegetable oil in a large sauté pan or skillet over medium-high heat. Brown the rabbit pieces, turning them with tongs, then remove from the pan and set aside.

Add the onions and mushrooms and sauté for 5 minutes. Add the tomatoes, bay leaves, and tomato paste, and cook 5 minutes longer over low heat. Add the wine and bring to a boil.

Return the rabbit to the pan, and bake uncovered for 45 minutes, turning the pieces after 20 minutes. Remove the rabbit from the sauce and place on a warm serving platter. Discard the bay leaves. Mix the butter with the remaining 2 tablespoons flour and add this bit by bit to the simmering sauce to thicken it. Pour the sauce over the rabbit, and serve.

NOTE: The dish can be prepared up to 2 days in advance and reheated, covered, in a 300°F. oven for 20 minutes, or until hot.

SERVES 4

ITALIAN
LITTLE
TOUCHES

*If entrées are the jacket and pants of a suit, then these recipes
are the accessories that make all the difference as to how
the ensemble looks. Most of these side dishes were conceived
by chefs as garnishes; however they are so delicious and
versatile that they deserve their own star billing as
recipes; the recipes they accompany are noted.*

*This chapter contains many wonderful vegetable and
carbohydrate side dishes, as well as some basic sauces used
frequently in this book. These are dishes that can become the
stars of the plate if the entrée is a simple piece of grilled protein.
Now that pasta and risotto have come into their own right, can
polenta be far behind? Every culture has its version of cornmeal
mush; it is fried into hush puppies in the southern United States,
called porridge in England, and polenta in Italy. It can be
creamy like a porridge, or it can be crusty and grilled.*

CAPONATA

BILLY VALENTINE, EAST HAMPTON, NEW YORK

Caponata is a sweet and sour Sicilian vegetable relish the chef serves with Grilled Veal Chops (page 141). However, it goes well with any simple grilled or broiled entrée, and can be served with greens underneath as a salad.

$^1/_2$ cup olive oil
4 tomatoes, peeled, seeded, and chopped (page 30)
$^1/_2$ yellow onion, peeled and minced
1 tablespoon minced garlic
Pinch of dried basil
Pinch of dried oregano
1 large eggplant, peeled and finely chopped
$^1/_4$ cup salt, plus more to taste
5 celery stalks, trimmed and finely chopped
1 cup green olives, drained, pitted, and finely chopped
1 cup pine nuts, toasted (pages 16–17)
$^1/_3$ cup red wine vinegar
$^1/_3$ cup sugar
$^1/_3$ cup water
Freshly ground black pepper

Heat ¼ cup of the olive oil in a heavy saucepan over high heat. Add the tomatoes, onion, garlic, basil, and oregano. Lower the heat and sauté for 15 to 20 minutes, stirring frequently, until the onions are soft. Remove the pan from the heat and set aside. Sprinkle the eggplant with the ¼ cup salt, toss, and place in a colander to drain for 20 minutes (a good bit of liquid will exude).

Fill a small pot with water, bring to a boil, and add the celery; blanch for 2 to 3 minutes. Drain and rinse under cold running water. Drain again and pat dry. Drain the olives and pat dry. Stir the celery and olives into the tomato mixture.

Thoroughly rinse the salt from the eggplant under cold running water and drain the eggplant well on paper towels. Heat the remaining ¼ cup olive oil in a medium sauté pan over high heat. Add the eggplant and sauté for 2 minutes, or until tender. Stir the pine nuts into the eggplant. Remove the mixture from the heat and set aside to cool. Combine the eggplant and tomato mixtures.

In a small saucepan over medium heat combine the vinegar, sugar, and water. Cook for 3 minutes, or until the sugar is dissolved. Remove from heat and set aside to cool.

Stir the vinegar mixture into the vegetables a bit at a time, until the desired consistency and flavor are reached; the caponata should be thick. Adjust the seasoning with salt and pepper and refrigerate.

NOTE: The caponata can be refrigerated for up to 5 days.

MAKES ABOUT 3 CUPS

CHEF'S TIP

Never cook eggplant in an aluminum pot; the eggplant will discolor.

BRUSCHETTA SPREAD

SETH RAYNOR, NANTUCKET, MASSACHUSETTS

With a glass of wine at night, there is nothing better than a slice of hearty toasted Italian bread spread with a robust topping, and this certainly meets that definition. The chef serves this as an accompaniment to Carpaccio of Sirloin (page 59), but bruschetta is delicious alone.

**3 red bell peppers, roasted, peeled, seeded, and chopped
  (pages 8–9)**
¹/₂ cup kalamata olives, pitted and chopped
1 tablespoon olive oil
Freshly ground black pepper
12 slices (each ¹/₂ inch thick) Italian bread, toasted

Combine the roasted bell pepper, olives, olive oil, and pepper in a small bowl, stir, and allow to rest for 15 minutes for the flavors to blend.

To serve, spread the bell pepper mixture thinly on the slices of toast.

NOTE: According to personal taste, a few cloves of crushed garlic or some fresh chopped rosemary or Italian parsley can be added to this spread.

MAKES 12 PIECES

CHEF'S TIP

Soak olives in olive oil to remove some of the salty taste. The olive-scented olive oil can then be used in salad dressing.

BAKED VEGETABLES

JOHN NEAL, NEW ORLEANS, LOUISIANA

The chef serves this colorful mélange of vegetables with Loin of Lamb with Garlic Sauce (page 148), but it would be wonderful with any simple entrée of meat, poultry, or fish. And it is as good at room temperature or chilled as it is hot.

2 small white onions, peeled and chopped
2 tablespoons garlic oil (available at specialty food stores)
4 Roma (pear) tomatoes, halved lengthwise, then cut into thin crosswise slices
2 zucchini, halved lengthwise, then cut into thin crosswise slices
2 tablespoons chopped fresh rosemary
Salt and freshly ground black pepper
Olive oil for drizzling

Preheat the oven to 375°F. Place a layer of onions on the bottom of four 4-ounce gratin dishes or 1 large gratin dish and drizzle with the garlic oil. Alternate layers of tomatoes and zucchini on top of the onions, seasoning each layer with rosemary, salt, and pepper; then drizzle everything with olive oil. Cover with aluminum foil and bake for 20 minutes, or until the vegetables are set.

NOTE: The dishes can be prepared for baking up to 1 day in advance and refrigerated. Bring to room temperature before baking.

SERVES 4

GRILLED VEGETABLES

FELIX STURMER, KANSAS CITY, MISSOURI

Grilled vegetables are a wonderful option in place of a salad. They can be served hot, at room temperature, or cold, and look beautiful on a buffet.

1 cup olive oil
1 sprig fresh rosemary, leaves removed and chopped
^{1}/$_4$ cup diced onion
2 garlic cloves, peeled and minced
Salt and freshly ground black pepper
2 zucchini, sliced ^{1}/$_2$ inch thick
1 red bell pepper, seeds and ribs removed, and cut into wedges
   (pages 8–9)
1 red onion, peeled and sliced ^{1}/$_3$ inch thick
6 unpeeled baby red potatoes, halved and boiled for 8 minutes

Combine the olive oil, rosemary, onion, garlic, salt, and pepper in a large mixing bowl. Add the vegetables and marinate for 30 minutes to 2 hours.

Light a charcoal or gas grill. When the coals are medium-hot, drain the vegetables and place them on the grill. Turn with tongs until cooked to desired doneness, and browned.

NOTE: The vegetables can marinate for up to 24 hours.

SERVES 6

CHEF'S TIP

An easy way to separate garlic cloves from the whole head is to pound the base of the head on the kitchen counter a few times; then it will be very easy to pull off individual cloves of garlic.

SAUTÉED VEGETABLES

TOM EMERICK, HOUSTON, TEXAS

This is a wonderful vegetable dish to serve with a dark entrée, since the colors are so bright. Any color of pepper can be substituted for those listed here.

2 tablespoons olive oil
1 yellow bell pepper, seeds and ribs removed and cut into thin
    strips (pages 8–9)
1 red bell pepper, seeds and ribs removed and cut into thin strips
    (pages 8–9)
1 green bell pepper, seeds and ribs removed and cut into thin strips
    (pages 8–9)
1/2 pound mushrooms, rinsed and sliced
1/2 pound thin asparagus spears, blanched in boiling water for 2
    minutes, and cut into 2-inch sections
2 tablespoons chopped fresh purple or green basil
Salt and freshly ground black pepper

Heat the olive oil in a large sauté pan or skillet and add the peppers and mushrooms, sautéing over medium heat until they are cooked but still retain some crispness. Add the blanched asparagus and the basil and season with salt and pepper. Serve immediately.

NOTE: The vegetables can be cut a few hours in advance and kept refrigerated. Do not sauté until just prior to serving.

SERVES 6

CHEF'S TIP

While basil cannot be frozen as leaves, since they will turn brown and lose flavor, they can be packed in olive oil and frozen in that manner. Pack some in ice cube trays so that you will have a few tablespoons every time you need them.

FRIED EGGPLANT

ROLAND HUET, NEW ORLEANS, LOUISIANA

Fried eggplant is a classic accompaniment to many Italian veal and chicken dishes. It can also be layered with spaghetti sauce and mozzarella cheese for an eggplant parmigiana.

1 large eggplant, about 1¹/₂ pounds
Salt and freshly ground pepper
All-purpose flour for dredging
4 egg whites
1¹/₂ cups milk
2 cups bread crumbs
2 to 3 cups peanut oil

Peel the eggplant and cut into long ¹/₂-inch strips. Place the eggplant in a colander and sprinkle the slices generously with salt. Place a plate on top of the eggplant, weight it with 5 pounds of cans, and allow the eggplant to drain for 30 minutes. Rinse the slices, and pat dry. Season the flour with salt and pepper. Dredge the strips in the seasoned flour.

Combine the egg whites and milk to make an egg wash. Dip the eggplant strips in the egg wash, then in the bread crumbs. (Make sure the strips are covered completely with breading.) Fill a deep pot with the peanut oil, and heat it to 375°F. Add the strips, turning them frequently, and fry until golden brown, about 5 to 6 minutes. Drain the slices on paper towels and serve immediately.

NOTE: The eggplant can be prepared for frying up to 2 hours in advance. Fry just prior to serving.

SERVES 4

BRAISED FENNEL

PATRICK CLARK, NEW YORK, NEW YORK

Chef Clark serves this fennel with a veal chop but it is delicious with any simple meat, poultry, or fish entrée.

3 tablespoons unsalted butter
¼ cup finely minced shallots
1 sprig fresh rosemary
1 star anise pod (available in Asian markets and most supermarkets)
2 medium fennel bulbs, trimmed and thinly sliced
1 cup chicken stock
Salt and freshly ground black pepper

Melt the butter in a medium sauté pan or skillet over medium heat. Add the shallots and sauté, stirring frequently, for 2 to 3 minutes, or until the shallots are soft. Add the rosemary, star anise, and fennel to the pan. Sauté for 2 to 3 minutes, or until the rosemary becomes fragrant and the fennel begins to wilt.

Add the stock and bring to a boil over high heat. Reduce the heat to medium, and cook the mixture for 4 to 5 minutes, or until the fennel is cooked but still has a slightly crunchy texture, and almost all the liquid has evaporated. Season with salt and pepper to taste, and serve immediately.

NOTE: The fennel can be prepared up to 2 days in advance and refrigerated, tightly covered. Reheat it, uncovered, over medium heat.

SERVES 4

CHEF'S TIP

Most recipes call for only the fennel bulbs, but do save the celerylike stalks. Sauté them and add to spaghetti sauce, or put them in a vase of water and they will perfume the kitchen.

BROCCOLI, ITALIAN STYLE

GOFFREDO FRACCARO, NEW ORLEANS, LOUISIANA

A hint of garlic, fruity olive oil, and Parmesan cheese give this broccoli a delicious flavor and aroma. The same treatment can be used with blanched asparagus or cauliflower.

1 bunch broccoli (about 3 heads)
3 tablespoons olive oil
1 teaspoon minced garlic
Salt and freshly ground black pepper
2 tablespoons freshly grated Parmesan cheese

Bring a large pot of salted water to a boil. Separate the broccoli florets and trim the tough skin from the stalks. Slice the stalks into $1/2$-inch pieces on the diagonal.

Have a bowl of ice water handy. Add the broccoli to the boiling water and cook for 6 to 8 minutes, until tender but resistant to the bite. Drain and plunge into ice water to stop the cooking action. Drain well.

Heat the olive oil in a large sauté pan and add the garlic. Cook over moderate heat for 1 minute and add the broccoli. Cook, tossing, for about 2 minutes. Season with salt and pepper, sprinkle Parmesan cheese over all, and serve immediately.

NOTE: The broccoli can be blanched up to 1 day in advance and refrigerated, tightly covered.

SERVES 4

CHEF'S TIP

Plunging green vegetables into ice water once they have been cooked sets their bright green color and also stops the cooking action so the vegetables do not get too soft.

SAUTÉED ESCAROLE

HALEY GABEL, NEW ORLEANS, LOUISIANA

While the chef serves this as a garnish to Sautéed Veal Chops (page 130), this simple sauté of tasty greens is excellent with any meat or poultry entrée.

2 tablespoons olive oil
2 tablespoons unsalted butter
1 teaspoon minced garlic
¹/₂ teaspoon crushed dried red pepper flakes
4 cups packed escarole leaves
Salt

In a medium sauté pan or skillet, heat the olive oil and butter with the garlic and crushed red pepper flakes. Add the escarole and toss until wilted. Add salt to taste. Serve immediately.

NOTE: The same treatment works well with chicory or radicchio.

SERVES 4

GRILLED POLENTA

FERNANDO SARACCHI, NEW ORLEANS, LOUISIANA

Polenta is one of those magical foods: It can be creamy and comforting right from the pot, or, if chilled and then grilled, it has a crusty surface similar to toast. It can be used like toast as a base for foods, such as the chef's Calamari with Spinach (page 50).

3 quarts water
3 tablespoons sea salt
2²/₃ cups (1 pound) polenta (coarse-ground cornmeal)
6 tablespoons (³/₄ stick) unsalted butter

Bring half the water to a boil in a very large saucepan. Add the sea salt. Mix the remaining water with the polenta, and pour it into the boiling water, stirring continuously with a whisk. Reduce the heat to low and cook about 25 to 30 minutes, stirring frequently with a wooden spoon; the mixture should be very thick.

Stir in 4 tablespoons (¹/₂ stick) of the butter. With the remaining 2 tablespoons butter, grease a jelly roll pan, and pour in the polenta while it is still very hot; let cool completely. When the polenta is cold, cut it into triangles and grill it over medium-hot coals until browned on both sides, about 3 minutes.

NOTE: The polenta can be prepared up to 2 days in advance and refrigerated, tightly covered. Grill it just prior to serving.

SERVES 4

CHEF'S TIP

While polenta is available at most specialty food stores, there is no reason that any coarsely ground yellow cornmeal cannot be used in its place at a fraction of the cost. Do not buy "instant polenta," since the granulation is too fine to grill well.

CREAMY POLENTA

RANDY WINDHAM, NEW ORLEANS, LOUISIANA

Every culture has its cornmeal mush, and polenta, now the rage in Italian restaurants, is that culture's version. It can serve as the base for any braised meat dish instead of potatoes or rice.

2 cups cold water
2 cups milk
1 cup polenta (coarse-ground cornmeal)
$^1/_3$ cup ($^2/_3$ stick) unsalted butter
$^1/_2$ cup freshly grated Parmesan cheese
Salt and freshly ground white pepper

In a large, heavy saucepan, stir the water, milk, and cornmeal together. Bring to a boil over medium heat, whisking constantly; the mixture will become lumpy as it comes to a boil, but the lumps will be beaten out. Cook over low heat until thick, stirring constantly, about 25 to 30 minutes. Stir in the butter and Parmesan cheese. Add salt and pepper to taste.

NOTE: The polenta can be made up to 4 hours in advance. Do not stir in the butter, but allow it to melt over the top of the polenta to prevent a skin from forming. Reheat the polenta gently, stirring in the butter, cheese, and salt and pepper at that time.

SERVES 4

POLENTA CAKES

CHARLES PALMER, NEW YORK, NEW YORK

The chef makes these cakes as a base for Sautéed Soft-shell Crabs (page 101); however they are excellent topped with anything from poached eggs with a sauce to a hamburger. The crème fraîche adds creaminess, while the frying gives the cakes a crisp exterior.

²/₃ **cup milk**
2³/₄ **cups chicken stock, preferably homemade (pages 26–28)**
Salt and freshly ground white pepper
1 box (13 ounces) instant polenta
¹/₄ **cup freshly grated Parmesan cheese**
¹/₃ **cup crème fraîche**
All-purpose flour for dusting
¹/₄ **cup clarified butter (page 11)**

Combine the milk, chicken stock, salt, and white pepper in a medium saucepan. Bring the mixture to a boil over high heat, and whisk in the instant polenta. Reduce the heat to low, and cook, stirring constantly, until the mixture has thickened, about 3 to 4 minutes. Add the cheese and crème fraîche, stirring well to incorporate. Continue cooking for 1 to 2 minutes. Remove the pan from the heat and spread the mixture on a greased baking sheet, spreading it to an even 1-inch layer with a rubber spatula.

Set aside until the polenta has cooled and hardened. When the polenta is at room temperature, cut out 8 circles with a 3-inch round cutter. Dust the circles lightly with flour on both sides and set aside.

To finish the dish, heat the clarified butter in a 10-inch sauté pan or skillet over medium-high heat. Place the reserved polenta cakes in the pan and sauté, turning once, until golden brown on both sides. Remove the cakes from the heat and hold until ready to serve.

NOTE: The polenta mixture can be prepared up to 2 days in advance and refrigerated, tightly covered. Dust the circles with flour and fry just prior to serving.

MAKES 8 CAKES

CHEDDAR POLENTA

TED FONDULAS, KILLINGTON, VERMONT

This version of polenta has some American overtones, since Cheddar cheese, rather than the usual Parmesan, is used. The polenta is formed in molds, which are easy to make and look special on any plate.

3 cups milk
2 tablespoons unsalted butter
1 cup cornmeal
³/₄ cup grated Cheddar cheese
Salt and freshly ground black pepper
¹/₂ teaspoon ground nutmeg
2 tablespoons olive oil

Put the milk and butter in a medium saucepan and bring to a boil over medium-high heat. Sift the cornmeal into the mixture, whisking vigorously. Stir for 5 minutes over low heat. Remove the pan from the heat and add the Cheddar cheese, stirring until incorporated. Add the salt, pepper, and nutmeg to taste.

While the mixture is still warm, spoon it into eight 4-ounce ramekins. Refrigerate about 2 hours, or until the polenta sets. To serve, preheat the oven to 350°F. Unmold the polenta ramekins, brush the tops with the olive oil, and bake for 10 minutes, until golden and warmed through.

NOTE: The polenta can be made up to 4 days in advance and refrigerated. Do not unmold or bake until just prior to serving.

SERVES 8

CHEF'S TIP

To keep leftover cheese from becoming moldy, rub the sides with an all-vegetable shortening such as Crisco before wrapping in plastic wrap.

POTATO GNOCCHI

TODD ENGLISH, CHARLESTOWN, MASSACHUSETTS

Gnocchi are small potato (or sometimes semolina) dumplings that are used in Italian cooking as an alternative to pasta. The chef uses these as a base for Wood-grilled Lobster with Toasted Walnuts (page 102), but they are versatile and can be tossed gently with any pasta sauce.

2 russet potatoes, peeled and cut into 1-inch chunks
1½ cups all-purpose flour, plus extra for dusting the work surface
3 egg yolks, lightly beaten
Salt and freshly ground black pepper

Put the potato cubes in a large saucepan and cover them with lightly salted water. Bring the water to a boil over high heat and cook the potatoes until soft, about 12 to 15 minutes. Drain them well in a colander. Dust a work surface with flour. Mash the potatoes through a ricer into a pile on the work surface. Add the egg yolks, salt, and pepper. Add the 1½ cups flour, a little at a time, and knead gently, only enough to incorporate.

On a floured surface, form a strip of dough ½ inch wide and 2 to 3 feet long. Cut the strip into ½-inch pieces, then roll the pieces into balls. Using 2 forks, roll the balls the full length of the fork prong, pressing to create a pocket in the middle with a fork mark at the end. Continue with the remaining dough and set the gnocchi aside.

Bring a large pot of salted water to a boil. Drop the gnocchi in the pot of boiling water and cook approximately 6 to 8 minutes, or until they rise to the surface.

NOTE: The gnocchi can be made 1 day in advance and refrigerated, tossed with cornmeal so they will not stick together.

SERVES 4

HERBED BOILED POTATOES

Sylvain Portay, New York, New York

Americans associate pasta or risotto with Italian cooking, but there is also a role for potatoes in both authentic Italian and Italian-inspired food. These buttery Yukon Gold potatoes take very well to the flavor of herbs.

2 pounds small Yukon Gold potatoes, about 1 1/2 inches in diameter
1 sprig fresh sage
1 sprig fresh rosemary
1 bay leaf
1 garlic clove, peeled and mashed
Salt and freshly ground black pepper
2 tablespoons unsalted butter

Scrub the potatoes and place them in a deep-sided saucepan with the sage, rosemary, bay leaf, and garlic clove. Fill the pan with cold water and salt the water lightly. Bring the potatoes to a boil over high heat, reduce the heat to medium-high, and boil until the potatoes are tender, about 12 to 15 minutes.

Allow the potatoes to cool in their cooking liquid, then drain well and slice into 1/4-inch slices; cover the slices with plastic wrap to prevent the potatoes from drying out.

Put the butter in a medium sauté pan and heat over medium-high heat. Add the potatoes and toss in the hot butter until they are warmed through. Remove the potatoes from the heat, season with salt and pepper, and serve immediately.

NOTE: The potatoes can be prepared up to the final heating up to 8 hours in advance and kept, covered, at room temperature.

SERVES 4

TOMATO SAUCE

Udo Nechutnys, St. Helena, California

There are as many versions of tomato sauce as there are cooks in the kitchen. This is a good all-purpose sauce with a pleasing consistency. For a more intense sauce, substitute red wine for the water.

2 tablespoons olive oil
1 medium onion, peeled and chopped
3 garlic cloves, peeled and minced
2 tablespoons all-purpose flour
2 sprigs fresh parsley
1 bay leaf
2 sprigs fresh oregano
1 sprig fresh thyme
1 sprig fresh rosemary
1 cup water
10 medium tomatoes, peeled, seeded, and chopped (page 30)
Salt and freshly ground black pepper

Heat the olive oil in a sauté pan over medium heat. Add the onion and garlic and cook 2 or 3 minutes, or until the onion is translucent. Sprinkle the onion mixture with the flour and cook over low heat for 2 minutes, stirring constantly. Add the parsley, bay leaf, oregano, thyme, rosemary, water, tomatoes, salt, and pepper and bring to a boil over medium-high heat. Reduce the heat, and simmer the sauce for 20 to 30 minutes, stirring occasionally. Discard the herb sprigs and bay leaf and purée the sauce in a blender or food processor fitted with the steel blade. Season with additional salt and pepper to taste.

NOTE: The sauce will keep up to 5 days, refrigerated, or it can be frozen for up to 3 months.

MAKES 2 1/2 CUPS

BASIC PESTO SAUCE

RANDY WINDHAM, NEW ORLEANS, LOUISIANA

What started as a pasta sauce has now become pesto passion, and this sauce can be used as a marinade, prior to grilling food, or as a sauce for everything from toast to tuna, not to mention pasta.

1 bunch basil, stemmed (about 1 cup of packed leaves)
3 garlic cloves, peeled
1¹/₂ tablespoons toasted pine nuts (pages 16–17)
1¹/₂ teaspoons salt
1 cup (4 ounces) grated Parmesan cheese
1 cup olive oil

In a food processor, purée the basil leaves, garlic, pine nuts, salt, and Parmesan cheese until smooth. With the motor running, add the olive oil in a slow, steady stream.

NOTE: Pesto keeps well for up to 1 week, refrigerated and tightly covered. It can also be frozen.

MAKES 1¹/₂ CUPS

CHEF'S TIP

In winter, when fresh basil is more difficult to find, substitute 1 cup of Italian parsley leaves and add 1 teaspoon of dried basil to make a sauce similar in flavor.

DESSERTS:

LA DOLCE VITA

Italian desserts tend to be simple, often based on the
succulent fruits of the country, treated to enhance their
natural glory. This chapter contains many such recipes that
can be completed in a matter of mere minutes.
There is a place, however, for a great cake or a dense,
rich chocolate dessert in the Italian repertoire as well
as in our own. While a few of these recipes may
seem complex, they have been broken into small
steps, none of which are difficult.

FIGS IN CABERNET SAUVIGNON WITH ALMOND ICE CREAM

Udo Nechutnys, St. Helena, California

Southern Italian cooking involves a lot of almonds from the North African influence centuries ago. This easy ice cream is satiny from the eggs, although it is made with milk and not cream, and the wine-marinated figs are an excellent complement.

Ice Cream
1 quart milk
1 cup sugar
10 egg yolks
1 teaspoon vanilla extract
$^1/_2$ pound blanched slivered almonds
$^1/_4$ cup amaretto

Figs
6 ripe figs
Sugar
1$^3/_4$ cups Cabernet Sauvignon or other dry red wine

To make the ice cream, bring the milk to a boil in a saucepan. Place the sugar and egg yolks in a large mixer bowl and beat well; add the vanilla. Add the milk to the sugar and eggs while whipping. Transfer the mixture to the top of a double boiler over hot water and beat until thick and doubled in volume. Remove from the heat, stir in the almonds and amaretto, and chill well. Process in an ice cream freezer according to the manufacturer's directions.

To prepare the figs, peel the figs, cut in half, and sprinkle the tops with sugar. Place in a flat bowl with the wine and marinate for at least 2 hours. Reserve the figs and marinade.

To serve, place 2 fig halves in each dish and top with ice cream. Drizzle the marinade over the ice cream.

NOTE: The ice cream can be made up to 2 days in advance and kept in the freezer. Allow it to soften for 30 minutes before serving.

SERVES 6

CHEF'S TIP

To use dried figs in place of fresh, select figs that are plump and not hard, and heat the wine almost to boiling. Halve and soak the figs in the hot wine to rehydrate.

RASPBERRY AND FIG GRATIN

JEREMIAH TOWER, SAN FRANCISCO, CALIFORNIA

Tangy sour cream is the perfect foil to the combination of raspberries and succulent fresh figs, but almost any combination of fruits would benefit from this same simple yet sophisticated treatment.

1 cup fresh raspberries
$^1/_2$ cup sour cream, thinned with 2 tablespoons milk
1 cup figs, peeled and halved
3 tablespoons firmly packed dark brown sugar

Preheat the broiler. Layer the raspberries in a gratin dish. Pour the sour cream over the raspberries and top with the figs. Sprinkle generously with brown sugar. Place the gratin dish under the broiler for 30 seconds to 1 minute, or until the sugar has melted and browned. Serve immediately.

NOTE: The gratin can be assembled a few hours in advance and refrigerated. Do not broil until just prior to serving.

SERVES 4

STRAWBERRIES ITALIAN STYLE

Adriana Giramonti, Mill Valley, California

The Italians are very fond of macerating fruit with wine as a simple ending to a meal. In addition to being served plain, this can also be served on top of ice cream.

3 quarts fresh strawberries
1 cup sugar
Juice of 2 lemons
Juice of 1 orange
¹/₂ cup sweet vermouth
1 cup white wine

Wash and hull the strawberries, and slice into medium-sized pieces. Place in a bowl and sprinkle the sugar over the fruit. Add the lemon juice, orange juice, vermouth, and wine. Mix gently and refrigerate at least 1 hour. Serve in chilled glass cups.

NOTE: This dish can also be done with ripe peaches, or some combination of peaches and berries.

SERVES 8

BERRIES AND AMARETTO CREAM

A N D R E A T R I T I C O , N E W O R L E A N S , L O U I S I A N A

This dessert is simultaneously rich and light. The almond-scented brown sugar sour cream is spooned over luscious fresh berries.

2 cups sour cream
¹/₃ cup packed brown sugar
¹/₄ cup amaretto
2 cups fresh strawberries, hulled and quartered
2 cups fresh raspberries

Place the sour cream, brown sugar, and amaretto in a bowl and mix until thoroughly blended; set aside.

Combine the strawberries and raspberries, and spoon into serving bowls. Top with the cream.

NOTE: The cream can be made up to 2 days in advance and refrigerated, tightly covered.

SERVES 6

CHEF'S TIP

If brown sugar has hardened, there are two remedies: Either place a few slices of fresh apple in the bag and seal tightly for 1 day, or place the sugar in a food processor, breaking up large lumps, and process until smooth.

BERRIES WITH SWEET MARSALA SAUCE

ANDRÉ POIROT, NEW ORLEANS, LOUISIANA

This is one of those blissfully easy recipes that goes from oven to table in the same dish. It is quick to make, and the perfect ending to a rich Italian meal.

SAUCE
6 tablespoons sugar
1 cup sweet marsala wine or sweet sherry, plus more for sprinkling
6 egg yolks

ASSEMBLY
4 slices (4 inches each) sponge cake or pound cake
1 cup sliced fresh strawberries
1 cup fresh raspberries
1 cup fresh blueberries
1 cup fresh blackberries
Fresh mint sprigs, for garnish

To make the sauce, preheat the broiler. Place the sugar, marsala, and egg yolks in a double boiler over barely simmering water; whisk until thickened and doubled in volume, about 3 to 4 minutes.

Arrange the slices of sponge cake in an ovenproof gratin dish, sprinkle with marsala, and scatter the berries on top. Cover the fruit with the sauce and place under the broiler, 3 to 4 inches from the heat, until golden brown, about 1 to 2 minutes. Garnish with mint sprigs and serve at once.

NOTE: The sauce can be prepared a few hours in advance and held at room temperature, and the cake and berries can be arranged at the same time. Broil just prior to serving.

SERVES 4

FRUIT GRANITA WITH POMEGRANATE SAUCE

G. Scott Philip, San Antonio, Texas

Granitas are Italian ices with a very granular texture, since they do not contain the egg whites used in French sorbets. This citrus granita is delicious with its bright red sauce.

Granita
2 pounds (8 cups) granulated sugar
1 quart water
3 cups pink grapefruit juice (from about 4 grapefruit)
2 cups unsweetened pineapple juice
1 cup freshly squeezed lime juice, plus grated zest of 3 limes (about 5 limes)
1/2 cup freshly squeezed lemon juice, plus grated zest of 1 lemon (about 3 lemons)
1/4 cup white tequila

Pomegranate Sauce
Seeds from 5 fresh pomegranates, white pith and skin discarded
1 cup water
5 tablespoons granulated sugar
1/4 cup crème de cassis
2 teaspoons arrowroot, dissolved in 1/4 cup cold water

For the granita, bring the sugar and water to a boil in a large saucepan and simmer for 5 minutes, or until the mixture has a syrupy consistency. Add the juices and zests to the syrup and allow to stand 10 minutes. Stir in the tequila and place the liquid in an ice cream freezer. Process according to manufacturer's instructions. Transfer to a bowl and place in the freezer.

To make the sauce, put the pomegranate seeds in a blender or a food processor fitted with the steel blade and purée. Pour into a saucepan, along with the water and sugar. Bring to a boil and add the crème de cassis and arrowroot mixture, stirring to mix well. Simmer until thickened, remove from the heat, strain to remove the seeds, and chill well.

To serve, spoon the sauce around the granita and splash some tequila on top, if desired.

NOTE: The granita can be made a few days in advance.

SERVES 8 TO 10

CHEF'S TIP

Select large, heavy pomegranates, which will have larger kernels and more juice. The skin should be shiny, not shriveled, and unbroken.

CRANBERRY-WALNUT CROSTATA

JOHANNE KILLEEN, PROVIDENCE, RHODE ISLAND

A crostata is a low Italian fruit tart baked flat on a pastry crust. With tart cranberries, this is not a sweet dessert, but the richness of the pastry gives a sensuous feel.

PASTRY

$^1/_2$ pound (2 sticks) unsalted butter, cut into $^1/_2$-inch cubes
2 cups all-purpose flour
$^1/_4$ cup superfine sugar
$^1/_2$ teaspoon kosher salt
$^1/_4$ cup ice water
Flour for dusting

FILLING

2 cups fresh cranberries (defrosted frozen cranberries may be substituted)
$^1/_2$ cup chopped walnuts, toasted in a 350°F. oven for 5 minutes
2 tablespoons confectioner's sugar, plus additional for garnish
2 tablespoons firmly packed dark brown sugar

To make the pastry, freeze the butter cubes on a baking sheet for 10 minutes. Place the flour, sugar, and salt in the bowl of a food processor. Pulse a few times to combine. Add the butter cubes, and toss with your fingers to coat each cube with the flour. Pulse quickly on and off 15 times, or until the butter particles are the size of small peas. Add the ice water through the feed tube, and pulse on and off until the dough is moist and holds together when a piece is pressed between your fingers. Do not let it become a solid mass.

Turn the contents of the bowl onto a sheet of aluminum foil and shape into a rough ball. Wrap the dough in foil and refrigerate for at least 2 hours, or until firm.

To complete the crostata, preheat the oven to 450°F. Roll the tart dough into an 11-inch circle on a lightly floured surface and transfer it to a baking sheet.

Combine the cranberries, walnuts, the 2 tablespoons confectioner's sugar, and the brown sugar in a mixing bowl. Toss to combine evenly. Mound the cranberry mixture in the pastry circle, leaving a 1½-inch border around the outside edge. Fold the dough border toward the center of the tart, letting the pastry drape gently over the fruit. Press down on the dough at the baking sheet, snugly securing the sides and the bottom. Without mashing the fruit, gently pinch the soft pleats of dough that form the draping.

Bake the tart in the preheated oven for 20 to 25 minutes, or until the crust is golden and the berries are juicy. Cool on a rack for 10 minutes, dust with confectioner's sugar, and serve warm, with crème anglaise or whipped cream if desired.

NOTE: The tart can be made up to 1 day in advance and kept at room temperature.

SERVES 6 TO 8

CHEF'S TIP

All pastry dough freezes well for up to 2 weeks. Defrost the wrapped dough on a counter for 30 to 45 minutes before rolling, or until it is still quite cold but pliable.

ZABAGLIONE SARAH VENEZIA

FRANCESCO ANTONUCCI, NEW YORK, NEW YORK

Zabaglione is one of the classic Italian desserts. It is a custard flavored with marsala wine that is usually served warm. In this version, the custard becomes enriched with a topping of vanilla ice cream.

8 egg yolks (or 10 yolks if using a cookie cutter to mold the dessert)
¹/₃ cup marsala wine
6 tablespoons sugar

GARNISH
1 pint vanilla ice cream
1 pint fresh raspberries
1 cup fresh strawberries
Fresh mint sprigs

Combine the yolks, wine, and sugar in a metal mixing bowl, and whisk well. Place the bowl in a pan of barely simmering water, and continue to whisk. Be certain that the water does not reach boiling temperature; if the water is too hot it will cook the eggs. Keep whisking the mixture over the heat to allow it to thicken. When the mixture has thickened enough so that whisking the yolks reveals the bottom of the bowl, take the zabaglione off the heat.

If you want the dessert to be in a shape, spoon the warm zabaglione into a cookie cutter of your choice placed flat on a plate (Francesco Antonucci used a 5-inch star cookie cutter). Allow the zabaglione to set up for 5 minutes in the mold. If the dessert is to be simply mounded on the plate, it only needs to rest for 2 minutes.

To serve, preheat the broiler. Place a scoop of vanilla ice cream in the center of the zabaglione. If you used a mold, remove it at this time. Put the plate in the oven and broil just until the zabaglione is lightly browned, about 30 to 45 seconds. Garnish with the fresh berries and mint sprigs and serve immediately.

NOTE: The zabaglione can be made up to 1 hour in advance and allowed to set up.

SERVES 6

SPICED PEARS WITH PORT AND GORGONZOLA

MICHAEL KORNICK, CHICAGO, ILLINOIS

Gorgonzola is perhaps the most robust and flavorful of the blue-veined cheeses, and this is a vividly colored, imaginatively flavored dessert.

POACHED PEARS
2 cups port wine
4 pieces star anise
4 cinnamon sticks
4 whole cloves
$1/4$ teaspoon nutmeg
$1/2$ teaspoon freshly ground black pepper
$1/4$ cup honey
$1/2$ cup firmly packed light brown sugar
4 ripe pears
$1/4$ cup ($1/2$ stick) unsalted butter

GARNISH
4 slices Gorgonzola cheese, 3 ounces each
1 cup toasted walnut halves

Heat the port to boiling in an ovenproof saucepan over medium heat, and add the anise, cinnamon sticks, cloves, nutmeg, pepper, honey, and brown sugar. Cook the mixture until the liquid is reduced by one-third.

Preheat the oven to 325°F. Peel, quarter, and core the pears. Heat the butter in a medium sauté pan or skillet over medium heat. Sauté the pears for 2 to 3 minutes. Add the pears along with the butter to the poaching liquid. Bake the pears in the oven for 20 to 25 minutes, or until they are tender.

To assemble the dish, place a slice of Gorgonzola cheese on each of 4 serving plates. Spoon the pears and some sauce next to the cheese. Garnish with the toasted walnut halves and serve.

NOTE: The pears can be poached up to 2 days in advance and refrigerated, tightly covered. Reheat them over low heat to warm before serving.

SERVES 4

POACHED PEARS WITH RAISIN FILLING

GUNTER PREUSS, NEW ORLEANS, LOUISIANA

Delicate poached pears with a vibrant raspberry sauce are a wonderful, low-fat ending to any meal. The Italian influence here is seen in the raisin and rum filling used in that country.

RAISIN FILLING
$^1/_4$ cup chopped raisins
1 teaspoon sugar
2 tablespoons dark rum

RASPBERRY SAUCE
2 cups whole raspberries
1 cup white wine
Juice of 1 lemon
$^1/_4$ cup sugar
1 tablespoon cornstarch mixed with $^1/_4$ cup cold water
2 tablespoons cherry brandy

PEARS AND POACHING LIQUID
4 ripe pears
1 cup white wine
1 teaspoon sugar
Juice and rind of 1 lemon
1 cinnamon stick
$^1/_2$ cup water

Mix the filling ingredients in a bowl and reserve. In a saucepan, simmer the raspberries, white wine, lemon juice, and sugar for 5 minutes. Add the cornstarch/water mixture and simmer for another 3 or 4 minutes. Strain the berries and add cherry brandy. Reserve.

Slice the bottoms off the pears. Peel the pears, and rub immediately with a sliced lemon to prevent discoloration. Remove the cores through the bottom, leaving the stems intact. Combine the wine, sugar, lemon juice and rind, cinnamon stick, and water in a large saucepan and bring to a boil. Add the pears and poach, covered, over low heat for 15 to 20 minutes, or until the pears are tender when pierced with a knife. Remove the pears, and drain standing upright. Chill, if desired.

To serve, stuff the pears through the bottom with the filling, stand upright on plates, and spoon the raspberry sauce around them.

NOTE: All components of this dish can be made up to 2 days in advance and refrigerated. Bring the sauce to room temperature before serving.

SERVES 4

MASCARPONE CHEESE MOUSSE WITH BERRIES

KILIAN WEIGAND, BOSTON, MASSACHUSETTS

This ethereal cheese mousse has the flavor of cheesecake, since the eggs are baked, and it is the perfect topping for fresh fruit.

1 package (8 ounces) cream cheese, softened
8 ounces mascarpone cheese (available at specialty stores, or see Mail Order Sources)
1 cup sugar
2 eggs
Zest of 1 lemon
1 tablespoon vanilla extract
$^1/_3$ cup heavy cream
3 to 4 cups berries (strawberries, blueberries, raspberries, blackberries, or some combination), cleaned, and stemmed or hulled if necessary
3 tablespoons fruit-flavored liqueur

PATRICK CLARK,
CHEF, TAVERN ON THE GREEN, NEW YORK, NY. FORMER CHEF, THE HAY ADAMS HOTEL, WASHINGTON, DC

Why did you become a chef?
My father was a chef with Restaurant Associates when they operated the Four Seasons and La Fonda del Sol in the 1960s, and my mother was a great cook, too.

How did you receive your training?
I went to New York City Technical College, but it was training with Michel Guérard in France that really set my style.

Any tips to pass on?
An easy way to get sections of citrus fruit is to cut off both ends so that the fruit sits flat on the counter. Then peel off the pith, using the natural shape of the fruit as a guide. You can then cut between the membranes and remove the sections.

Preheat the oven to 350°F., and place a kettle of water over high heat to bring it to a boil. Beat the cream cheese, mascarpone, and sugar with an electric mixer until light and fluffy, add the eggs, and beat until smooth. Scrape down the sides of the bowl and add the lemon zest and vanilla. Scrape the batter into a greased 9-inch cake pan, then place the cake pan in a roasting pan. Place the roasting pan in the oven, and pour enough boiling water into the pan to come halfway up the sides of the cheesecake pan. Bake for 20 to 30 minutes, or until a knife inserted in the center comes out clean.

Carefully remove the pan from the roasting pan, and when it cools to room temperature, transfer it to the refrigerator and chill completely. (Turn off the oven and allow the boiling water to cool before removing the pan, or remove it very carefully to avoid being burned.)

To serve, scrape the cheesecake into a mixing bowl and beat in the cream; it should have the consistency of a thick pudding. Place the berries in a bowl and toss with the liqueur. Divide the berries among serving bowls, and top with the cheese mixture.

NOTE: The mousse can be prepared up to 3 days in advance and refrigerated, tightly covered.

SERVES 6 TO 8

CASSATA PARFAIT TORTE

WARREN LE RUTH, BAY ST. LOUIS, MISSISSIPPI

This is the perfect dessert for a dinner party, since it has to be made at least the night before, and looks far more complicated than it really is to make. The candied fruits in the frozen custard filling add texture as well as flavor. Start the cassata a day before serving.

CAKE
4 eggs
$1/3$ cup sugar
$1/4$ cup all-purpose flour
2 tablespoons cocoa
$1^1/2$ tablespoons cornstarch
2 teaspoons grated lemon zest

FILLING
$1^1/2$ cups whipping cream
4 egg yolks
$1/3$ cup powdered sugar
1 teaspoon vanilla extract
1 teaspoon grated lemon zest
$1/4$ cup finely chopped glacéed fruits

In a bowl, mix the eggs and sugar. Heat over hot water, stirring constantly, to 110°F. Take the pan off the heat and beat for 8 to 12 minutes on high speed with an electric mixer until very light and fluffy.

Preheat the oven to 350°F. Sift the flour, cocoa, and cornstarch together 3 times. Carefully fold the flour mixture and lemon zest into the egg mixture. Pour into a greased and floured 9-inch cake pan. Bake in the preheated oven until set and springy, about 25 to 30 minutes. Remove the cake from the oven and invert it onto a cooling rack.

To make the filling, whip the cream to stiff peaks and refrigerate. In the bowl of an electric mixer, whip the egg yolks, sugar, and vanilla for 7 to 9 minutes on high speed until very light. Add the lemon zest, and gently fold the egg yolk mixture and glacéed fruits into the whipped cream.

To assemble the cake, cut wax paper into 2 circles, each 9 inches in diameter. Fit the circles into the bottoms of two 9-inch cake pans, and divide the filling evenly between the pans. Cut the cake laterally into 2 layers, and place one on top of the filling in each pan.

Cover the pans with plastic wrap and freeze overnight. To serve, unmold so that the filling is on the top, and peel off the wax paper. Cut into slices and garnish with more whipped cream, if desired.

NOTE: For a change of flavor, rum extract can be added instead of the vanilla.

SERVES 10

CUSTARD CUPS WITH STREGA

GOFFREDO FRACCARO, New ORLEANS, LOUISIANA

These satiny custards are napped with an aromatic Italian liqueur, Strega, which means witch *in Italian. It is bright yellow in color and has the flavors of both vanilla and anise.*

4 eggs
1 1/2 cups sugar
1/2 teaspoon vanilla extract
1 teaspoon lemon zest
2 1/2 cups milk, scalded
3 tablespoons water
1/2 cup Strega liqueur

With an electric mixer, beat the eggs with 1/2 cup of the sugar and the vanilla until frothy and lemon-colored. Add the lemon zest and continue beating. Add the milk, whisking all the while. Boil the remaining 1 cup sugar with the water over high heat until the mixture caramelizes and turns brown, swirling the pan by the handle as the sugar mixture begins to change color. Divide the mixture among 6 custard cups, swirling to coat the bottoms.

Preheat the oven to 350°F. and bring a kettle of water to a boil. Fill custard cups with the custard mixture, and place them in a roasting pan. Fill the pan with enough boiling water to come halfway to the top of the cups. Bake for 45 minutes, or until a toothpick comes out clean when inserted into the center of the custards. Unmold and serve with Strega as a sauce.

NOTE: The custards can be made up to 1 day in advance and refrigerated. Do not unmold until just before serving.

SERVES 6

CHOCOLATE PÂTÉ

JOYCE BANISTER, NEW ORLEANS, LOUISIANA

A fine quality chocolate, such as Callebaut or Valhrona, is the crucial element in making this easy dessert a show-stopper for a dinner party. In classic Italian cooking, bits of broken butter cookies are added to the dense chocolate mixture. It adds a nice textural contrast.

2¹/₂ **pounds bittersweet chocolate, chopped (pages 10–11)**
1¹/₂ **cups (3 sticks) sweet butter, cut into 1-inch pieces**
¹/₂ **cup Chambord (raspberry liqueur) or amaretto**
1 **cup water**
4 **egg yolks, beaten**

Line a small loaf pan with plastic wrap to form a mold.

In a double boiler over barely simmering water, melt 2 pounds of the chocolate and the butter, with the Chambord and water, stirring until smooth. Set aside and let cool slightly.

Whisk the egg yolks into the cooled chocolate mixture. Strain through a fine-meshed sieve into the mold, cover, and chill.

To serve, melt the remaining ¹/₂ pound of chocolate in a double boiler over barely simmering water, stirring until smooth. Dip a large knife into hot water and cut the pâté into 1-inch slices. Decorate each serving plate with swirls of melted chocolate. Place a slice of pâté on each plate and serve.

NOTE: The pâté can be made up to 3 days in advance and refrigerated, tightly covered. Allow it to sit for 30 minutes before cutting.

SERVES 8

AMARETTO CHOCOLATE CAKE

WARREN LE RUTH, BAY ST. LOUIS, MISSISSIPPI

This is a classic layer cake, with a chocolate ganache filling and a basic lemon-scented sponge cake sprinkled with heady amaretto as the base.

CAKE
7 eggs
²/₃ cup sugar
³/₄ cup all-purpose flour
3 tablespoons cornstarch
2 teaspoons grated lemon zest

FILLING
3 cups heavy cream
6 ounces semisweet chocolate, chopped (pages 10–11)
¹/₄ cup amaretto

Preheat the oven to 350°F. Grease and flour two 9-inch-round cake pans.

To make the cake, mix the eggs and sugar in a bowl. Heat over hot water to 115°F., beating until doubled in volume. Sift the flour and cornstarch together 3 times. Carefully fold the flour, cornstarch, and lemon zest into the egg mixture. Pour into the prepared pans and bake for 25 to 30 minutes, or until a cake tester inserted into the center comes out clean. Allow to cool for 5 minutes on a cooling rack, and then turn out the cakes from the pans to the racks and cool completely.

To make the filling, heat the cream to 180°F. Stir in the chocolate and remove from the heat. Stir to melt, then refrigerate until chilled. Put 1 cake layer on a serving plate, and sprinkle with half of the amaretto. Whip the cream mixture until stiff. Spread ¼ of the cream mixture (filling) on the cake layer. Add the top layer of cake and sprinkle with the remaining amaretto. Ice the top and sides of the cake with the remaining chocolate filling, reserving some of it to pipe through a pastry bag for finishing decorative touches.

NOTE: The cake can be made up to 1 day in advance and refrigerated. Allow it to reach room temperature before serving.

SERVES 8 TO 12

WHITE CHOCOLATE MOUSSE IN AN ALMOND COOKIE SHELL

MASATAKA KOBAYASHI, SAN FRANCISCO, CALIFORNIA

White chocolate makes a natural pairing with nuts; and this mousse is made with an Italian meringue base (with a sugar syrup beaten into the egg whites) to create a smoother texture.

COOKIES
3 egg whites
2 tablespoons sugar
2 tablespoons all-purpose flour
$^1/_2$ cup sliced almonds, toasted (pages 16–17)

MOUSSE
1 cup sugar
$^1/_2$ cup water
8 egg whites
6 egg yolks
1 tablespoon white rum
1 pound white chocolate, melted

Preheat the oven to 350°F. To make the cookies: Beat the egg whites briefly; add the sugar and flour, then whisk. Stir the almonds into the mixture. Butter a sheet pan and spoon tablespoons of the mixture onto the pan. Spread slightly with the back of a spoon to form circles about 2 inches apart. Bake for 5 to 7 minutes. Remove from the oven, and while the cookies are still hot, mold them into small cups by pressing them over a rolling pin. Set aside to dry.

To make the mousse, boil the sugar and water to 240°F. on a candy thermometer, or until the mixture forms a soft ball when a bit is dropped into ice water. In the large bowl of an electric mixer, beat the egg whites at medium speed until foamy, then increase the speed to high and beat until stiff peaks form. Slowly add the sugar syrup, and beat until glossy.

Put the egg yolks in a metal bowl and beat over simmering water with a whisk. Add the rum to the egg yolks and continue to beat until thick. Gently fold the egg yolks into the beaten egg whites. Fold the melted chocolate into the egg mixture. Refrigerate at least 4 hours. Serve 1 scoop of mousse in each almond cookie shell.

NOTE: The cookies can be made up to 2 days in advance and kept in an airtight container, and the mousse can be made up to 2 days in advance and refrigerated, tightly covered.

SERVES 6

MAIL ORDER SOURCES

While ingredient availability is certainly greater than at any time in our history, from time to time there may be items that are either difficult to locate or it's more fun to have them sent. Here is a list of companies I use, and what they offer:

Aidells Sausage Company
distributed by Williams-Sonoma
P.O. Box 7456
San Francisco, CA 94120-7456
800-541-2233

Bruce Aidells creates a superb line of traditional and creative cooked and uncooked sausages.

American Spoon Foods
P.O. Box 566
Petoskey, MI 49770
800-222-5886

Chef Larry Forgione and his partner Justin Rashid carry a wonderful line of dried fruits and other ingredients for cooking, as well as many American regional specialties from other companies.

Auricchio Cheese, Inc.
5810 Highway NN
Denmark, WI 54208
414-863-2123

An excellent importer of fine Italian cheeses from fresh mascarpone to Parmesan.

Balducci's
11-02 Queen's Plaza South
Long Island City, NY 11101-4908
800-225-3822

This famed New York gourmet market has gone mail-order, with everything from fresh pastas and excellent sauces to prime meats and desserts. Get on the mailing list; it's like having the shop next to your phone.

Broken Arrow Ranch
P.O. Box 530
Ingram, TX 78025
800-962-4263

Mike Hughes was the pioneer of farm-raised game in Texas, and his venison and other products are superb.

Dallas Mozzarella Company
2944 Elm St.
Dallas, TX 75226
800-798-2954

Paula Lambert's superb line of Italian and Texas-style cheeses.

D'Artagnan
399-419 St. Paul Ave.
Jersey City, NJ 07306
800-327-8246

The only source for fresh foie gras, as well as great game birds and meats, sausages, fresh poultry, as well as a line of superb pâtés and terrines.

The Farm at Mt. Walden
Box 515
The Plains, VA 22171
800-64T-ROUT

This small smokehouse in the Shenandoahs makes the best smoked trout I've ever eaten, as well as a hot-smoked salmon.

Nantucket Off-Shore Seasonings
P.O. Box 1437
Nantucket, MA 02554
508-228-9292

A wonderful line of preblended, salt-free herb and spice rubs to put on foods before grilling.

Rossi Pasta
P.O. Box 759
Marietta, OH 45750
800-227-6774

Excellent flavored dried pastas.

Santa Barbara Olive Company
P.O. Box 1570
Santa Ynez, CA 93460
800-624-4896

The best olives produced domestically, although all are brine-packed, plus excellent olive oil.

Summerfield Farms
10044 James Monroe Highway
Culpepper, VA 22701
703-547-9600

One of the country's best lines of game meats and birds, plus free-range veal that has more flavor than the paler cuts, lamb, organ meats, and already-made glace de veau.

Timber Crest Farms
4791 Dry Creek Rd.
Healdsburg, CA 95448
707-433-8251

Excellent nuts and dried fruits from raisins to papayas.

INDEX
